Liebe Schülerin, lieber Schüler,

in deinem Workbook findest du nicht nur **Übungen**, sondern auch **Checkpoint-Seiten**, **Selbsteinschätzungsseiten**, **Activity pages** und ein kompaktes **Grammar File**.

Ampel

Am Ende einer Übung befindet sich eine Ampel.

Wenn du eine Übung gemacht hast, male die Ampel so aus:

Die Übung war leicht zu lösen: Male den unteren Kreis **grün** aus.	Die Übung war nicht so leicht zu lösen: Male den mittleren Kreis **gelb** aus.	Die Übung war schwer zu lösen: Male den oberen Kreis **rot** aus.

Vor einer Klassenarbeit kannst du dir die Übungen, die du gelb oder rot markiert hast, noch einmal anschauen und wiederholen.

Checkpoint

Auf den Checkpoint-Seiten kannst du selbst testen, wie gut du schon in Englisch bist.

Die Lösungen der Checkpoint-Aufgaben findest du hinten auf den Seiten 78–83.

Die rechte Spalte der Lösungsseite gibt dir Lernhilfen, falls du Schwierigkeiten mit den Aufgaben hattest.

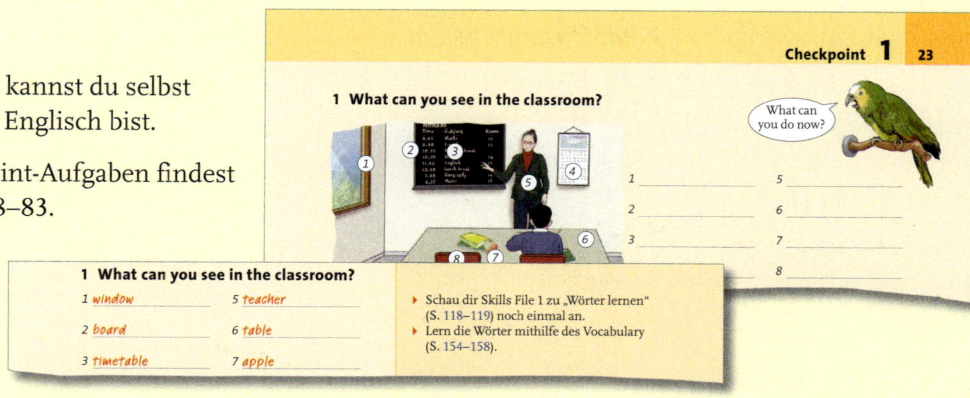

Selbsteinschätzung

Auf den Selbsteinschätzungsseiten gibst du an, was du schon in Englisch kannst.

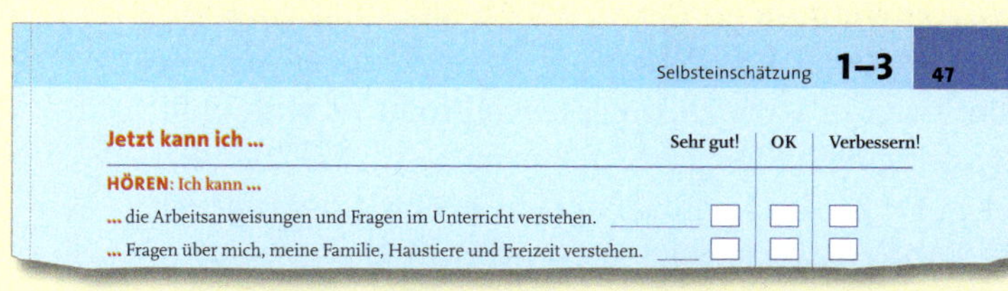

Grammar File *kompakt*

Falls du eine Frage zur Grammatik hast, während du eine Aufgabe löst, kannst du hinten in deinem Workbook auf den Seiten 84–88 nachschlagen.

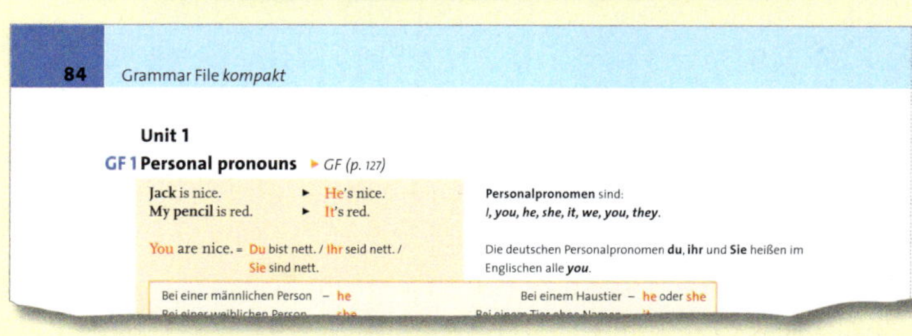

Audio-CD

Der rote Kopfhörer zeigt dir, dass du dir etwas auf der Audio-CD anhören kannst.

e-Workbook

Im e-Workbook findest du zusätzliche interaktive Übungen.
Der Zahlencode (Quick Code) links neben der Übung verweist auf die passende Aufgabe im e-Workbook.

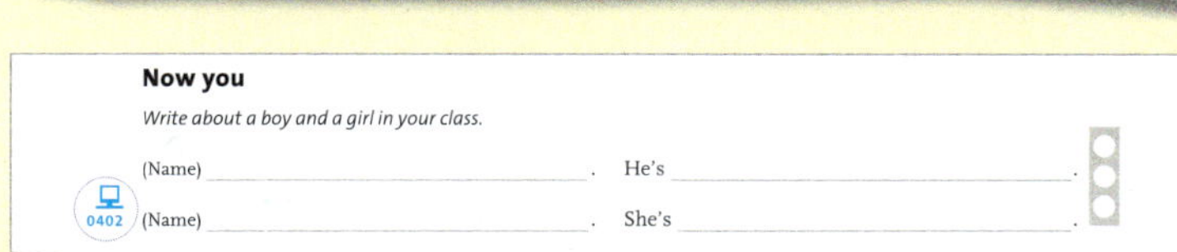

English G 21 • 2. Fremdsprache
Band A 1 • Workbook

Im Auftrag des Verlages herausgegeben von
Prof. Hellmut Schwarz, Mannheim

Erarbeitet von
Jennifer Seidl, M.A., München

unter Mitarbeit von
Bernard Brown, Holzkirchen (Activity pages)

in Zusammenarbeit mit der Englischredaktion
Kirsten Bleck (Projektleitung); Filiz Bahsi (verantwortliche Redakteurin); Dr. Christian von Raumer; Julie Colthorpe; Susanne Bennetreu (Bildredaktion); Gareth Evans *sowie* Britta Bensmann

Beratende Mitwirkung
Susan Abbey, Nenagh, Irland; Bernhard Hunger, Dettingen; Angela Ringel-Eichinger, Bietigheim-Bissingen; Gabriele Rotter, Wiesbaden; Karl Starkebaum, Diekholzen

Illustrationen
Andreas Mack/blatteins, Freiburg
Johann Brandstetter, Winhöring/Kronberg (S. 66)
Katharina Wieker, Berlin (Activity page 3/4)

Layoutkonzept und technische Umsetzung
Korinna Wilkes; galindo • medien & gestaltung - berlin

Umschlaggestaltung
Klein und Halm Grafikdesign, Berlin

Bildquellen
Alamy, Abingdon (S. 37 Bild 5: Alaska Stock LLC; S. 48 Bild 9: CheapShots); Baker, York (S. 31 Dave); Bank of England, London (Activity Page 2 banknotes, reproduced with kind permission); Britta Bensmann, Berlin (S. 37 Bild 1 u. 4); Cinetext, Frankfurt/M. (S. 65 oben: Concorde u. Mitte: RR); Corbis, Düsseldorf (S. 60 sports shop: RF); Corel Library (S. 35 Bild 3–6; S. 37 Bild 2 u. 3; S. 48 Bild 2 u. 11; S. 49 Bild 2; S. 60 pool, soccer); Cornelsen Archiv, Berlin (S. 48 Bild 3, 7, 8; S. 49 Bild 3); Rob Cousins, Bristol (S. 4; S. 8 Ananda, Sophie, Dan u. Jo, Jack; S. 20; S. 44; S. 60 Jo, Sophie u. Emily, Jack, Ananda); David Dore, Guilford (S. 23; S. 35 Bild 1 u. 2); Gareth Evans, Berlin (S. 31 Kate u. Simon); Angelika Fischer, Berlin (S. 37 Bild 6); Ingram Publishing, UK (S. 48 Bild 1, 5, 6, 10; S. 49 Bild 4); Ute Klaphake, London (S. 48 Bild 4 u. 12); John Lally, York (S. 37 Bild 7; S. 48 Bild 13 u. 14); Norbert Schäfer Archiv, Düsseldorf (S. 31 oben); Jennifer Seidl, München (S. 8 Tim u. Becky, Florian; S. 31 Cathy, Tim, Becky, Lucy; S. 43; S. 49 Bild 1 u. unten; S. 54; S. 60 Becky u. Lucy, Tim u. Florian); Visum, Hamburg (S. 60 pet shop: pixsil.com)

Nicht alle Copyrightinhaber konnten ermittelt werden; deren Urheberrechte werden hiermit vorsorglich und ausdrücklich anerkannt.

Inhalt

www.cornelsen.de
www.EnglishG.de

1. Auflage, 1. Druck 2007

Alle Drucke dieser Auflage sind inhaltlich unverändert und können im Unterricht nebeneinander verwendet werden.

Druck: Himmer AG, Augsburg

ISBN 978-3-06-031073-9

Inhalt gedruckt auf säurefreiem Papier aus nachhaltiger Forstwirtschaft.

1 Hello, Emma! ▸ p. 8

a) *Read and write.*

Hello. My name is Emma.
I'm 12 years old. I'm from Bristol.
My favourite colour is red. Yes, red.

1 What's your name?
2 How old are you?
3 Where are you from?
4 What's your favourite colour?

YOU

1 My name ______________________

______________________.

2 I'm ______________

______________ old.

3 I ____________ from

______________________.

4 My ______________________

is ______________________.

b) *Write questions.*

1 name/What's/your ? ______________________

2 you/How/old/are ? ______________________

3 you/Where/from/are ? ______________________

0301
0302 *4* your/colour/What's/favourite? ______________________

2 New names

▸ p. 8

a) *Write.*

1 This *is Polly.* ____________

2 This ____________.

3 ____________

4 ____________

5 ____________

b) *Match and write.*

She's 11 years old. | They're twins. | She's new in Bristol. | She's 11 years old. | They're from Bristol. | He's from Bristol. | They're 12 years old. | She's from Bristol. | He's 11 years old.

1 Write about Ananda. ____________

2 Write about Jack. ____________

3 Write about Dan and Jo. ____________

____

4 Write about Sophie. ____________

Now you

Write about a boy and a girl in your class.

(Name) ____________. He's ____________.

0402 (Name) ____________. She's ____________.

3 WORDS What can you see? ▸ p. 9

a) *Write the correct numbers in the box.*

(1) boat ( ) kite ( ) water ( ) trees ( ) skateboard
( ) football ( ) house ( ) boy ( ) girls ( ) boys

b) *Write the words.*

I can see a b o a t and w _ _ _ _ and two g _ _ _ _ with a _ _ _ _.

I can see two _ _ _ _ with a _ _ _ _ _ _ _ _ and a _ _ _ with a red _ _ _ _ _ _ _ _ _ _.

I can see a _ _ _ _ _ and three _ _ _ _ _ too.

c) *Write correct words.*

0503
0504

t b a o ____________ b l f o t o l a ____________

a t r e w ____________ b s o a t r d k e a ____________

4 WORDS A word kite ▸ pp. 10–11

Find and write.

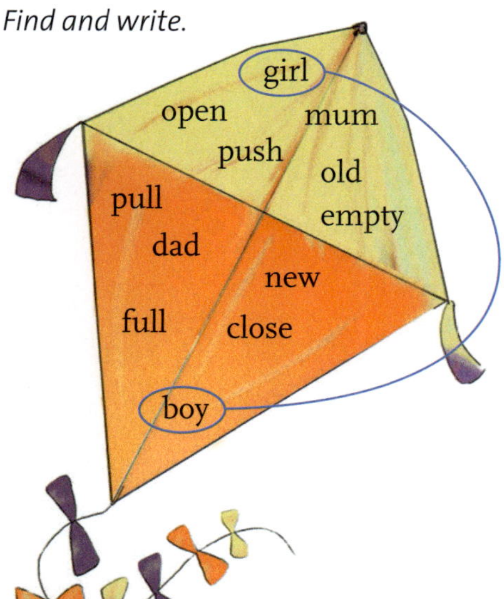

girl	boy
____________	____________
____________	____________
____________	____________
____________	____________
____________	____________

5 WORDS Dan's school shopping list ▸ p. 12

a) *Match and write.*

shopping		book
pencil		list
school		case
exercise		bag
glue		stick
pencil		tip
felt		sharpener

0605

! Two words.

shopping list

___

___

___

___

___

___

b) *Draw and write the names of four things from your school bag.*

1 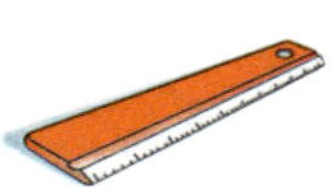

ruler

2 ___

3 ___

4 ___

5 ___

6 WORDS Colour words ▸ p. 13

Find and colour the colour words.

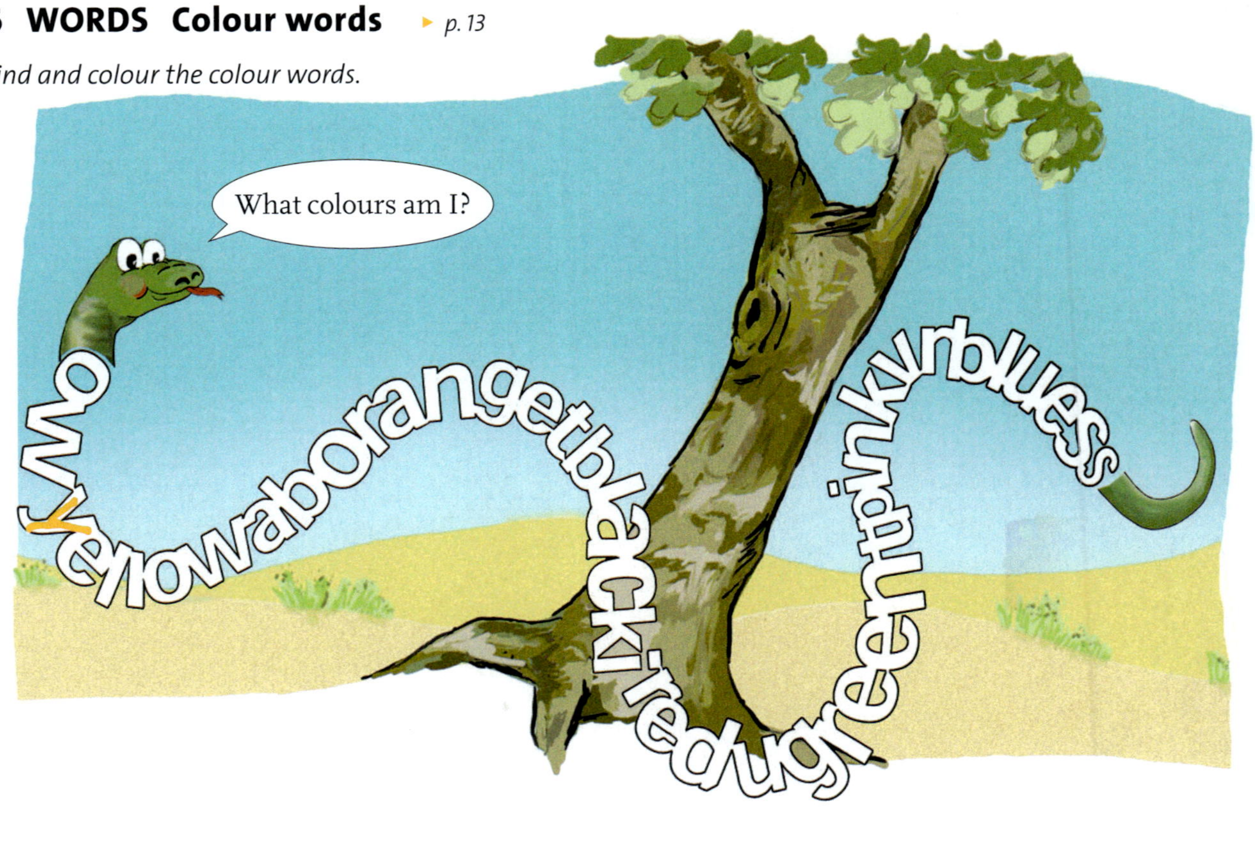

7 Prunella's plates ▸ p. 13

What colours are Prunella's plates? Write the colours.

blue

0707

Rhyme time*

* *Zeit für einen Reim*

One plate, two plates,
Three plates, four.
Five plates, six plates,
Two plates more[1].
Seven plates and one
Are eight.
Crash! Bang! Wallop!
My favourite plate ...
Aaaaw!

Now you

What's your favourite colour? It's ______________.

What colour is your school bag? ______________

What colour is your pencil case? ______________

What colour is your glue stick? ______________

8 What day is it? ▸ p. 14

Write the day. Look at the pictures and Jo's diary[2].

It's Monday.

M – badminton
T – pizza with Dad
W – football
T – shopping with Dad (new football?)
F – party
S – help Dad in house
S – new DVDs!!

[1] more [mɔː] *mehr* [2] diary ['daɪəri] *Terminkalender*

9 Find the house numbers ▸ p. 15

○ ***a)*** *Match six house numbers to the speech bubbles. Write the correct numbers from the box.*

Ananda

My house number is thirteen. ____

I live at number seventeen. ____

Sophie

We live at number seven. ____

Dan and Jo

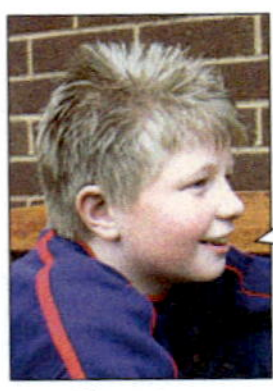
Florian

I live at number forty-two. ____

Tim and Becky

We live at number twenty-four. ____

My house number is twenty-eight. ____

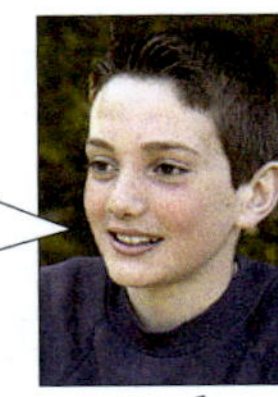
Jack

b) *Now write the red house numbers in words.*

0809

____

10 Who am I? ▸ p. 15

○ ***a)*** *Read the secret code[1] and write the letters in the speech bubble.*

37	36	35	34	33	32	31	30	29	28	27	26	25	24	23	22	21	20	19	18	17	16	15	14	13	12
A	B	C	D	E	F	G	H	I	J	K	L	M	N	O	P	Q	R	S	T	U	V	W	X	Y	Z

__ __   __ __ __ __   __ __   __ __ __ __ __ __ __ __ .

__ __ __ __ , __   __ __ __ __   __ __ __ __ ?

Start here:

twenty-five thirteen twenty-four thirty-seven twenty-five thirty-three
twenty-nine nineteen thirty-six thirty-seven twenty twenty-four thirty-seven thirty-six
thirty-seven nineteen fifteen thirty thirty-seven eighteen nineteen thirteen
twenty-three seventeen twenty twenty-four thirty-seven twenty-five thirty-three

b) *Write your answer in code. Write the numbers in words.*

My name is very nice.

____

____

____

[1] secret code [siːkrət ˈkəʊd] *Geheimcode*

11 What's the time? ▸ pp. 16–17

Draw the time on the clocks.

It's seven o'clock. It's quarter to five. It's half past ten. It's quarter past four.

It's five twenty-five. It's four thirty-six. It's twelve o two.

12 Prunella's clocks ▸ pp. 16–17

Look at Prunella's clocks. Write the times.

1 It's ______________________________. 4 ______________________________

2 ______________________________ 5 ______________________________

3 ______________________________ 6 ______________________________

One clock is right. Which clock is it? – Clock number ___ ___ ___ ___ is right.

Now you

0912

What's the time now? It's ____.

13 WORDS S-words ▸ p. 17

Read and write.

1 Can you sing a ...?
2 The Kapoors live in a flat over a ...
3 *Dilip*: Ananda is my ...
4 The ... holidays are great.
5 ... is the last day of the week.
6 Day six of the week is ...
7 I can see a boy with a red ...

1 s *o* *n* *g*
2 s _ _ _
3 _ _ _ _ _ _
4 _ _ _ _ _ _
5 _ _ _ _ _ _
6 _ _ _ _ _ _ _ _
7 _ _ _ _ _ _ _ _ _ _

0913
0914

Unit 1 New school, new friends

1 WORDS What's in the picture? (there is/are) ▸ p. 18–19

○ ***a)*** *Write the names of the things.*

1 ___ ___ ___ ___ ___ ___ [ ] ___ ___

6 [ ] ___ ___ ___ ___ ___ ___ s

7 [ ] ___ ___ ___ ___ s

8 ___ ___ ___ ___ [ ] ___ ___ ___ ___ s

4 ___ [ ] ___ ___ ___

9 ___ ___ [ ] ___ s

5 ___ ___ ___ [ ] s

2 ___ ___ ___ ___ ___ ___ ___ ___ [ ] ___

3 ___ ___ ___ ___ ___ [ ] ___ ___ ___ ___ ___

b) *Make a new word with the letters from the blue boxes in a). What is it? Write it in the speech bubble.*

c) *Look at the picture again. What is there? Write sentences with* **there is** *or* **there are**.

1 *There's a school bag.*

2 ______

3 ______

4 ______

5 *There are two books.*

6 ______

7 ______

8 ______

1000
1001
9 ______

2 WORDS Day one

▸ p. 20

Write words from the boxes.

students	year	
nervous	twins	first
welcome	Room	

w e l c o m e to the new school!

It's day one of the new school ___ ___ ___ ___ .

The new ___ ___ ___ ___ ___ ___ ___ ___ are at school.

Lessons are in ___ ___ ___ ___ 14.

Before lessons the ___ ___ ___ ___ ___ , Dan and Jo, are ___ ___ ___ ___ ___ ___ ___ .

Dan: You go ___ ___ ___ ___ ___ , Jo. – *Jo:* No, you.

3 He, she, it, ... (Personal pronouns)

▸ p. 20 • GF 1 (p. 127)

Match and colour.

HE	SHE	IT	THEY	
mum and dad	brother	girl	Ananda	Sophie
classroom	Dan and Jo	Jo	Mr Shaw	Mrs Kapoor
Prunella	colour	twins	dad	students
1103 school	pen	name	books	Jack

Rhyme time

School bag,
Pencil case,
Glue stick too.
First day of school for me,
What about you?

4 Hello! (Personal pronouns)

▸ p. 21 • GF 1 (p. 127)

Write I, you, he, she, it, we or they.

Jo Hello. My name is Jo, and this is my brother Dan. We're twins.

Florian Hi. My name is Florian.

Dan Florian? ______'s a German[1] name, right? Is your dad German?

Florian Yes, ______'s from Essen.

Dan Is your mum German too?

Florian No, ______'s English. ______'s from Bristol.

______'re very happy in Bristol. ______'s a nice place.

Sophie Hello. ______'m Sophie. Oh, ______'re new in Bristol too.

Florian Hi, Sophie. ______'m Florian. That's Dan and that's Jo. ______' re twins.

Teacher Ah, hello. ______'re the new students. Well, this is Room 14.

______'s a nice room. Let's go.

[1] German ['dʒɜːmən] *deutsch*

5 I'm Dan (Personal pronouns + be: positive and negative statements) ▸ p. 21 • GF 1–2a (p. 127–128)

a) *Complete with short forms: I'm, you're, he's, she's, it's, we're, you're, they're.*

1 ____________ Dan and Jo Shaw, right? But who is who?

2 ________ Dan and ________ Jo.

3 This is my sister Emily. ________ at Cotham too. ________ a very big school.

4 ______ in Room 14, right? Where are Emily and her friends?

5 ________ in Room 22.

b) *What's wrong? Correct the sentences. Write short forms.*

1 Toby is ten years old.

He isn't ten years old. He's eight years old.

2 It's half past eight.

____

3 Jack and Ananda are at the B&B.

____

4 Jo is in Room 14.

____

5 Polly is fifty years old.

____

6 'Dan, you're from London, right?'

Wrong. ______________________________

1205

6 Questions and answers (be: questions and short answers) ▸ p. 21 • GF 2b–c (p. 128)

Write questions and short answers.

1 Prunella/a/Is/poltergeist?

Is Prunella a poltergeist? ______ *Yes, she is.* ______

2 Mr Kapoor/from Uganda/Is?

______ ______

3 a parrot/Sheeba/Is?

______ ______

4 Jack/twelve/and/Ananda/Are?

1306 ______ ______

7 WORDS A puzzle ▸ p. 22

Write the words in the puzzle, then find the word in the pink boxes.

1 Please ... me your names.
2 ... please.
3 *Mr Kingsley:* It isn't a joke. Please, don't ...
4 *Ananda:* I can't play football, but I can play ...
5 And ... are you? What's your name?
6 Write your name on the board, ...
7 You're in ... 7PK.

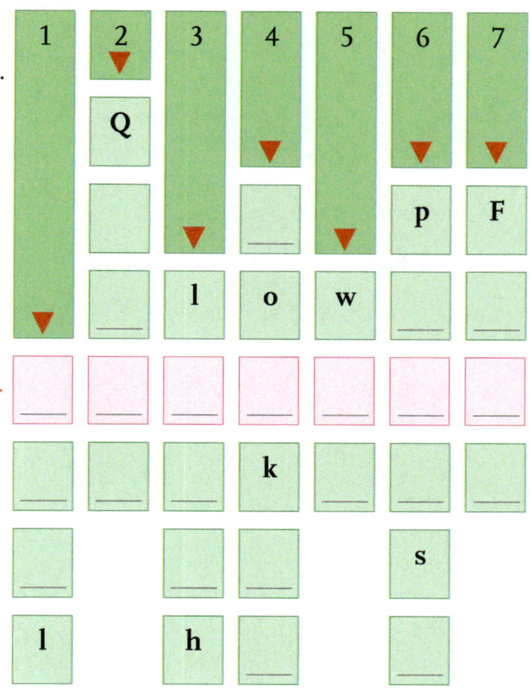

Who is your English __ __ __ __ __ __ __?

My ______

______.

○ 8 Can you do this? (can/can't) ▸ p. 22 • GF 3a (p. 129)

*Write sentences with **can** or **can't**.*

1 

I ______ draw a ______

2 

I ______ throw a big ______

3 

I ______ take my ______ to school.

4 

I ______ ______ my teacher on the ______

9 What can they do? (can/can't) ▸ p. 22 • GF 3a (p. 129)

Can or can't? Write sentences.

He • She • They	can can't	play hockey • see Polly • help in the shop • talk • *sing* • see Prunella

1 

She can't sing.

2 

3 

4 

5 

6 

1409

10 WORDS School subjects ▸ p. 23

Find the school subjects in the '?'. Write the subjects under the correct pictures.

Science

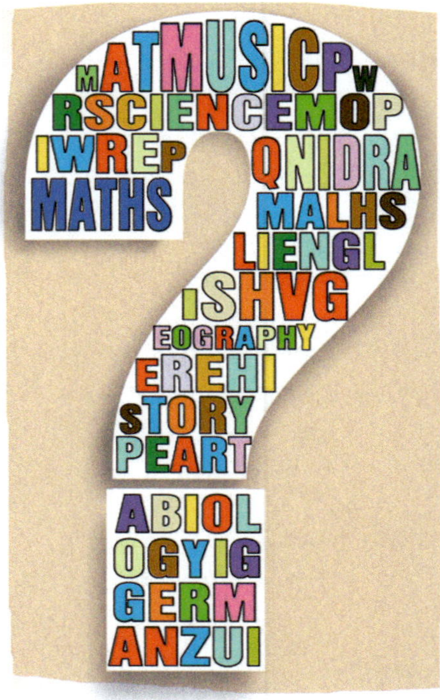

Now you

Look at your timetable.

1 What's lesson 1 on Monday?

It's ______________________.

2 What's lesson 2 on Wednesday?

____

3 What's after the first break on Tuesday?

____

4 What's the last lesson on Friday?

____

5 What's your favourite subject?

____

11 WORDS Where are the school words? ▸ p. 23

a) *Find and write the school words.*

p	b	r	e	a	k	b	S	l
s	o	j	k	y	s	o	c	e
M	a	t	h	s	u	o	i	s
y	r	w	q	p	b	k	e	s
v	d	s	f	e	j	x	n	o
m	p	u	h	l	e	d	c	n
F	o	r	m	l	c	s	e	s
M	u	s	i	c	t	w	m	q
t	i	m	e	t	a	b	l	e
j	p	t	e	a	c	h	e	r

1511

▶	▼
break	*board*
______	______
______	______
______	______
______	______
______	______

b) *Fill in words from a).*

1 We can play football in the *b r e a k*.

2 Can you __ __ __ __ __ 'favourite', please?

3 Are you in __ __ __ __ 7PK?

4 Jo, write 'Science' on the __ __ __ __ __, please.

5 English __ __ __ __ __ __ __ are great.

6 My favourite __ __ __ __ __ __ __ is English.

7 Is PE on Monday? – Look at the __ __ __ __ __ __ __ __ __.

Just for fun*

* *Nur zum Spaß*

A: 'Poltergeist' is a long word. Can you spell it, please?
B: Yes, I can. P-O-L ...
A: Wrong. It's I-T!

12 Please, Polly! (Imperatives) ▸ p. 23 • GF 4 (p. 130)

Complete the sentences.

be (2x) • sing • stop • talk • drop • eat • play

1

Mrs Hanson: Polly, be quiet, please! Don't talk!

2

Jack: Polly, ______ my apple! It's for school.

3

Jack: Please ______ ______ my felt tips, Polly.

4

Jack: Polly! ______ with my mobile phone!

5

Jack: Ouch!! ______ that, Polly. ______ nice.

6

Mr Hanson: Polly! It's six o'clock on Sunday morning. Please ______ now!

1612

13 WORDS Lists ▸ p. 23

Write the words in three lists.

throw	write	nervous	laugh	quiet	listen	lunch
student	wrong	meet	marmalade	white	timetable	think
climb	breakfast	clever	friend	great	come	

VERBS
throw, write, ______

ADJECTIVES
nervous, quiet, ______

NOUNS
lunch, ______

1613

14 STUDY SKILLS Wörter lernen

▸ *p. 23 • SF 1 (pp. 118–119)*

a) *Schau dir in deinem Buch das Vocabulary zu Unit 1 auf den Seiten 154 bis 158 gut an. Es ist viel mehr als eine Wortliste. Welche Informationen findest du dort?*

Überlege gut und mach ein Häkchen (✓) in die entsprechenden Kästchen:

Im Vocabulary finde ich ...

- ..., wie ich ein Wort aussprechen muss. ☐
- ..., wie ich ein Wort betonen muss. ☐
- ... Grammatikregeln. ☐
- ... Paare von Gegensätzen. ☐
- ..., wie ich Aufsätze schreiben kann. ☐
- ... nützliche Beispiele. ☐
- ... Hinweise auf Fehlerquellen. ☐

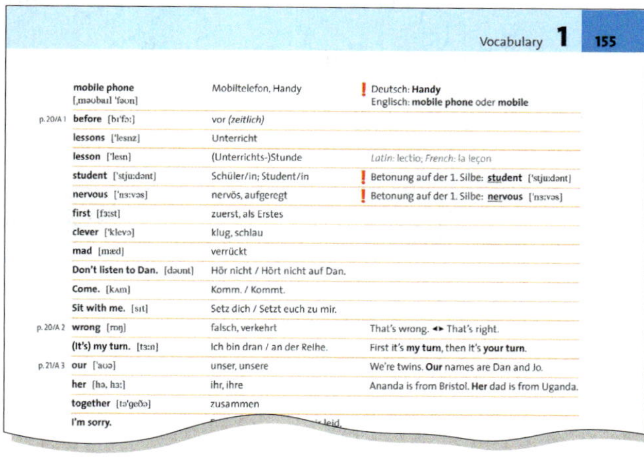

Vocabulary 1 155

	mobile phone [ˌməʊbaɪl ˈfəʊn]	Mobiltelefon, Handy	! Deutsch: **Handy** Englisch: **mobile phone** oder **mobile**
p. 20/A 1	**before** [bɪˈfɔː]	vor *(zeitlich)*	
	lessons [ˈlesnz]	Unterricht	
	lesson [ˈlesn]	(Unterrichts-)Stunde	*Latin:* lectio; *French:* la leçon
	student [ˈstjuːdənt]	Schüler/in; Student/in	! Betonung auf der 1. Silbe: **stu**dent [ˈstjuːdənt]
	nervous [ˈnɜːvəs]	nervös, aufgeregt	! Betonung auf der 1. Silbe: **ner**vous [ˈnɜːvəs]
	first [fɜːst]	zuerst, als Erstes	
	clever [ˈklevə]	klug, schlau	
	mad [mæd]	verrückt	
	Don't listen to Dan. [dəʊnt]	Hör nicht / Hört nicht auf Dan.	
	Come. [kʌm]	Komm. / Kommt.	
	Sit with me. [sɪt]	Setz dich / Setzt euch zu mir.	
p. 20/A 2	**wrong** [rɒŋ]	falsch, verkehrt	That's wrong. ◂▸ That's right.
	(It's) my turn. [tɜːn]	Ich bin dran / an der Reihe.	First it's **my turn**, then it's **your turn**.
p. 21/A 3	**our** [ˈaʊə]	unser, unsere	We're twins. **Our** names are Dan and Jo.
	her [hə, hɜː]	ihr, ihre	Ananda is from Bristol. **Her** dad is from Uganda.
	together [təˈgeðə]	zusammen	
	I'm sorry.	... leid.	

b) *Suche im Vocabulary auf der Seite 155 ...*

1 *... ein englisches Wort, das dem deutschen Wort ähnelt, aber anders betont wird:*

____

2 *... zwei englische Wörter, die Gegensätze sind:*

____

3 *... einen Hinweis auf eine Besonderheit, bei der man leicht einen Fehler machen kann (!):*

____

15 WORDS New words

▸ *p. 23*

*Make new words from the **green** words. Find eight or more words.*

teacher: *cat, eat,* ____________________

badminton: *to,* ____________________

timetable: ____________________

16 Meet Tom and his family.

a) Complete with: ***have/ has got***

1

I've got ________ a dog.

2

I ________ cat.

3

My brother ________ a dog.

4

My mother ________ a computer.

5

My brother and I ________ a big room.

6

Our mum and dad ________ a small room.

17 What have they got? (have got/has got) ▸ p. 24 • GF 5a (p. 130)

Complete with: ***have got, has got (✓), haven't got, hasn't got(✗)***

	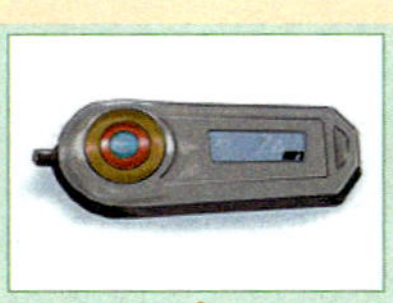			
Ananda	✓	✓	✓	✗
Dan	✗	✓	✓	✓
Jo	✗	✗	✓	✓

Ananda has got a mobile phone. She hasn't got a pet, but she 's got ________ lots of books.

Dan and Jo ________ pets, but they ________ an MP3 player.

Jo ________ lots of books, but he ________ a mobile phone. Ananda and Dan ________ lots of books. One student ________ an MP3 player. Who is it?

1817

18 Questions and answers (have got/has got)

▸ p. 24 • GF 5b–c (p. 131)

*Write questions with **have got/has got**. Then write short answers: **Yes, she has. / ... / No, they haven't. / ...***

1 Sophie/a sister?

Q: *Has Sophie got a sister?* A: *Yes, she has.*

2 Ananda/a brother?

Q: ____ A: ____

3 Sophie/a parrot?

Q: ____ A: ____

4 the Hansons/a B&B?

Q: ____ A: ____

5 Dan and Jo/a dog?

Q: ____ A: ____

Now you

Write short answers.

1 Have you got a sister? ____

2 Has your friend got a brother? ____

3 Have you got a pet? ____

4 Has your friend got a pet? ____

19 *Is* or *has*?

▸ p. 24 • GF 2a (p. 128), GF 5a (p. 130)

Write the sentences in the correct group.

She's got lots of pets.	*He's eleven.*	It's nice here.	She's got a dog.
He's in Form 7PK.	Where's Jo?	Who's got a B&B?	It's got six rooms.

's = is	's = has
He's eleven.	*She's got lots of pets.*

1919

20 PRONUNCIATION *a* [ə] or *an* [ən]? ▸ p. 24 🎧 2

*Say the words with **a** or **an** and write them in the correct list. Then listen to the CD and check your lists.*

- nice day
- idea
- apple
- yellow pen
- newspaper
- old picture
- empty room
- joke
- orange bag
- uniform
- exercise
- new word

a	an
a nice day	an idea
____________	____________
____________	____________
____________	____________
____________	____________
____________	____________

2020

21 PRONUNCIATION *the* with [ə] or [i]? ▸ p. 24 🎧 3

*Say the words with **the** and match them to the right box, **green** or **red**. Then listen to the CD and check.*

the first day the old school the uniform the orange book

the empty house the nice picture the MP3 player

the English teacher

[with ə]

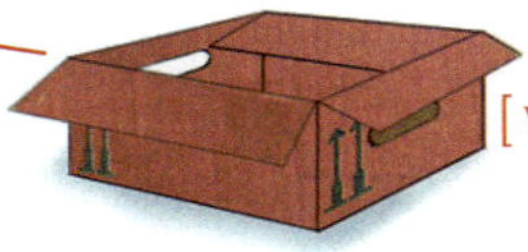

[with i]

the new girl

22 About you ▸ p. 24

*First read about Jo. Then write about you. You can change the **green** words.*

My name is Jo. I'm twelve years old and I'm from Bristol. I'm a student at Cotham School. My English teacher is Mr Kingsley. My favourite subject is PE. I can play basketball, but I can't play tennis. I've got a brother. I haven't got a sister, but I've got lots of nice friends.

My name is ______________________________

____

____

____

____

____

____

____

____

2022
2023

23 READING Meet the Baxters ▸ p. 34

a) *Read about Tim, Becky and Barnabas.*

Hello, I'm Tim Baxter. I'm eleven years old and I'm in Form 7SB. School is OK. My favourite subject is Science. I can't spell or do French, but I can do Maths and play badminton. I can climb trees too.
My favourite day is Saturday. I've got lots of comics in my room – in my school bag too. I've got a sister, Becky – well, Rebecca really, and a great pet, Barnabas.

Hi, I'm Becky. Tennis is great. I can play tennis, but I can't do tricks or climb trees. I've got lots of posters in my room. Tim is my little brother. He's nice, clever too. Oh, I'm thirteen and I'm in Form 8JW. My favourite subject is Art. My favourite day is Saturday.

Hello. My name is Barnabas – not 'Barney', please. Tim is my friend. I'm his pet. Tim is eleven. Me too. Becky is nice, but Tim is very nice.
Well, I can .., I can ... sit on the skateboard. I can't play badminton, but I can play CDs. My favourite show is 'Super Cat'. Cats are great. But parrots aren't great. Polly is not my friend. Oh, and my favourite day is – ermm – Sunday!

b) *What's right? Check the text and find out.*

	Tim	Becky	Barnabas
How old?	11/12/10	11/12/13	9/10/11
Form	7SB/8JW/7PK	8JW/7SB/7PK	–
Can ...	spell/do Maths/ do French	do tricks/play tennis/ climb trees	sit on the skateboard/ play badminton
Favourite day	Saturday/Friday/Sunday	Monday/Sunday/Saturday	Saturday/Sunday
Favourite subject	RE/Science/French	Art/English/RE	–
Has got ...	lots of comics/ lots of books	lots of posters/ lots of photos	a friend/a pet

● ***c)*** *Right or wrong? Correct the wrong sentences.*

1 Tim can play badminton. Right.

2 Barnabas is ten years old. Wrong. He's eleven years old.

3 Tim has got lots of football posters. ______

4 Becky can do tricks. ______

5 Becky is fourteen. ______

6 Barnabas can play CDs. ______

24 Months of the year ▸ p. 35

You can write eight months of the year with the letters. Which months are they?

A B C D E F H J L M N O R T U Y

____

____

2224

25 Find the month ▸ p. 35

Write down the letters from the boxes. Then find the correct month.

My first is in red. F or D

My second is in blue. ____ or ____

My third is in green. ____ or ____

My fourth is in brown. ____ or ____

My fifth is in purple. ____ or ____

My sixth is in yellow. ____ or ____

My seventh is in pink. ____ or ____

My eighth is in white. ____ or ____

26 Prunella's birthday calendar ▸ p. 35

Write the dates of the birthdays.

Emily – 01. 06.
Toby – 03. 07.
Hannah – 22. 10.
Sophie – 26. 03.
Sheeba – 21. 05.

Emily's birthday is on 1st June.

Toby's birthday ______________________.

Hannah's birthday ______________________.

Sophie's birthday ______________________.

Sheeba's birthday ______________________.

Now you

When's your birthday? My ______________________.

When's your friend's birthday? My friend's ______________________.

1 What can you see in the classroom?

1 ____ 5 ____

2 ____ 6 ____

3 ____ 7 ____

4 ____ 8 ____

2 Complete.

1 

Barnabas ____ a parrot.

He ____ a cat.

2 

'I ____ a very nice pet.

I ____ a mad cat!'

3 

They ____ classmates.

They ____ brother and sister.

3 Write what they *have got* and what they *haven't got*.

1 The Hansons ____ a B&B. It ____ five rooms.

2 The Kapoors ____ a house. They ____ a flat and a shop.

3 Ananda ____ a brother, but she ____ a pet. 20 points

Now you

First read about a new friend. Then write to the new friend about you.

Hi!

I'm your new friend from Australia. My name is Leo and I'm 12 years old. I've got a sister, Kim. She's 14. I can play tennis and football too.
My favourite subject is Science. I like History too. I've got lots of nice friends.
What about you?
Please write!

Hi!

I'm your new friend from Germany. My name is ____

____

____

____

____

____

2304
2305

Unit 2 A weekend at home

1 WORDS Tim's room ► p. 36

a) *Label the things in the pictures.*

bed • chair • desk • lamp • photos • shelf • wardrobe • window

(1) ____________

(2) ____________ (3) ____________ (4) ____________ (5) ____________

(6) ____________ (7) ____________ (8) ____________

b) *Now read about Tim's room. Is it picture 1 or picture 2?*

My room is white – oh, and orange, my favourite colour. You can see houses and the park from my window. There's a bed, a desk and a chair and there's a big wardrobe. I can throw all my things in there. There's a big poster and a photo of Barnabas. There's a shelf for books, CDs and school things and there's a lamp on my desk. I've got a computer and lots of great games. I'm happy with my room. It's really nice.

2400
2401

Tim's room is ____________________.

c) *Now read about Tim's room. Is it picture 1 or picture 2?*

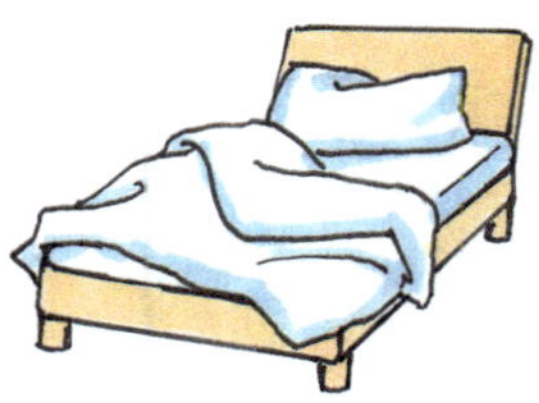

1 ____________ *2* ____________ *3* ____________ *4* ____________

2 REVISION *be* ► p. 36 • GF 2 (p. 128)

Look at exercise 1 *again. Write short answers: Yes, it is. / No, ...*

Is Tim's room white and orange? ____________________

Is his chair blue? ____________________

Is Barnabas in Tim's photos? ____________________

Are all Tim's CDs on his shelf? ____________________

Rhyme time

My room isn't big,
My things aren't new,
My bed is old,
My wardrobe too.
My desk is red,
My lamp is blue.
I ♥ my room,
What about you?

3 WORDS Pets ▸ p. 37

Label the pets.

budgie • cat • dog • fish • guinea pig • hamster • horse • mouse • rabbit • tortoise • parrot

1 

2 

3 

4 

5 

6 

7 

8 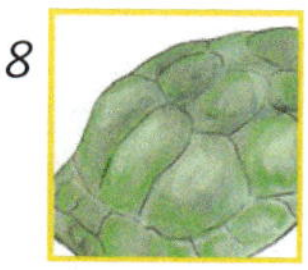

9 

10 

11 

2503

4 REVISION Where the Bristol pets live (have got/has got) ▸ p. 37 • GF 5a (p. 130)

a) *What is it? Label the pictures.*

1 

2 

3 

Rhyme time

A budgie, a guinea pig,
A tortoise too.
I've got lots of pets,
What about you?

b) *What have the pets got? Write sentences.*

Polly Bill and Ben Hip and Hop Sheeba Harry	have got has got	a hutch a cage a basket	... bedroom. ... living room. ... kitchen. ... garden.

Polly *has got a cage in the living room.*

Bill and Ben ______________________.

Hip and Hop ______________________.

____

____

5 PRONUNCIATION Plurals

▸ p. 38 • GF 6 (pp. 131–132) 4

Listen to the words. Then colour the last letters red, green or blue.

Look:

[-s]	[-z]	[-ɪz]
cats	girls	houses

classes

kites · pets · hands · days

baskets · windows · flats · jokes · pages

tortoises · horses · lessons · numbers

6 A day in the life of ... (Simple present: positive statements)

▸ p. 38 • GF 7a (pp. 132–133)

a) *Complete with words from the box.*

get up (2x) • help • meet • go • make • have • read • talk • think • work

Ananda: Mum, this is my essay for Mr Kingsley. It's about a day in my life. Listen, please, and tell me what you think.

I ______ at 7.30 every morning. My mum and dad ______ at 6.30. They ______ in our shop. We ______ breakfast together at 7.45. I ______ tea and toast for all the family. My mum and dad ______ the newspapers. My brother Dilip and I ______ about school and friends. Every morning we ______ in the shop and then we ______ to school. Before lessons I ______ my friends. Then I ...

2606

Oh, no, no, no! This essay is boring! I can't read this at school ...

b) *What's wrong with this essay? Write the sentences again with the green words in the right place.*

I go to bed at 7.30 in the morning. First, I have lunch. Then I wash my face and clean my teeth in the kitchen with my mum. At school we play football in Room 14. At 12.40 we all have breakfast at school. After school we have lessons in the park.
I get up at 9.30 in the evening.

I get up ______

______

______

______

______

______

______

______

7 STUDY SKILLS Mindmaps

▸ p. 38 • SF 3 (p. 121)

*Make a mind map about **My Saturday** in your exercise book.*
You can use these ideas:

write e-mails · read in bed · get up late · evening · go to bed at … · night · *morning* · *afternoon* · meet my friends · go to the shops · have breakfast · play football · listen to CDs · play with my pet · have lunch · clean my teeth · go to the park · wash my face

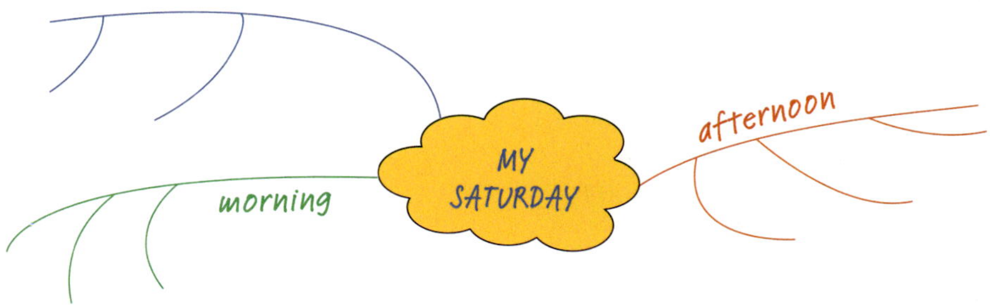

2707
2708

8 -s, -es or -ies? (Simple present: 3rd person singular)

▸ p. 39 • GF 7b (p. 133)

Write the verbs from the box in the correct lists.

> *clean* • *go* • *hurry* • listen • tidy • push • sleep • try • eat • wash • watch

-s: *cleans,* ______

-es: *goes,* ______

-ies: *hurries,* ______

9 Becky's weekends (Simple present: 3rd person singular)

▸ p. 39 • GF 7b (p. 133)

Write sentences about Becky's weekends.

1 

get up – 9 o'clock

2 
go to the shops

3 
play tennis – park

4 
watch TV – her family

5 
help mum – kitchen

1 On Saturdays she *gets up at 9 o'clock.* ______

2 Before lunch *she* ______.

3 In the afternoon ______.

4 In the evening ______.

2709 5 On Sunday ______.

10 Sundays (Simple present: positive statements)

▸ p. 39 • GF 7a–b (pp. 132–133)

a) *Put the words in the right boxes.*

I • You • We • Lots of boys and girls	My friend
______	______
______	______
______	______
______	______

has a small breakfast • eat lots of toast • like Sundays • reads comics • goes to the park • watch TV • play in the garden • eats toast • go to places • likes Sundays • listens to music • have a big breakfast

b) *Complete Sophie's text.*

First we have (have) breakfast together in the kitchen. Mum makes (make) tea and toast. Dad ______ (eat) lots of marmalade. Toby ______ (like) milk. After breakfast we ______ (go) to the park with Sheeba. Emily ______ (go) too. Then we ______ (help) Mum with lunch. Well, Dad ______ (watch) TV, or he ______ (read) his newspapers. After lunch Hannah and Sheeba ______ (sleep). Emily ______ (talk) to all her friends on her mobile phone. In the evenings we ______ (listen) to music or we ______ (watch) TV. I really ______ (like) Sundays.

2810

○ 11 WORDS Find the right word

▸ p. 40

Match two fish, colour the fish, then write one new word.

newspaper, ______

______

12 Right or wrong? (Simple present: negative statements)

► p. 40 • GF 7c (p. 134)

Mark the sentences right (√) or wrong (x). Write sentences with **don't** *for the wrong sentences.*

1 All pets need water. ✓

2 Horses live in hutches. ✗ Horses don't live in hutches.

3 Horses eat apples. ______

4 Hamsters like marmalade. ______

5 Rabbits eat fish. ______

6 Dogs go to school. ______

7 Cats drink tea. ______

8 Parrots need food. ______

2912

13 We're all different!

a) *Write 6 sentences.*

My mum		meat.	1 ______
My dad		toast.	2 ______
My brother	doesn't like	dogs.	3 ______
My sister		cats.	4 ______
My teacher		football.	5 ______
My friend		...	6 ______

b) *Find and circle the correct word.*

1 My dog (doesn't/don't) like meat.
2 I (doesn't/don't) play football.
3 My friend (doesn't/don't) like Tatort.
4 My sister and I (doesn't/don't) read comics.
5 Tim (doesn't/don't) go to the park.
6 You (doesn't/don't) live in England.
7 My mum (doesn't/don't) feed my hamster.
8 My rabbit (doesn't/don't) like carrots.

14 What Prunella does (Simple present: positive and negative statements)

▸ p. 40 • GF 7 (pp. 132–134)

Write about Prunella. Write about what she does (✓) and what she doesn't do (✗).

1) She talks to Sophie. 2) She doesn't like Emily.

____

____

____

____

____

○ 15 WORDS Family words

▸ p. 41

Put the family words from the box in the right list. Which words go together?

aunt • brother • daughter • father • grandma • grandpa • mother • sister • son • uncle

mother	father

Now you

Write about your family. Have you got brothers or sisters? Have you got grandparents, aunts, uncles and cousins?

I've got a ____

____

____

16 Who are they? (Possessive form)

▸ p. 41 • GF 9 (p. 135)

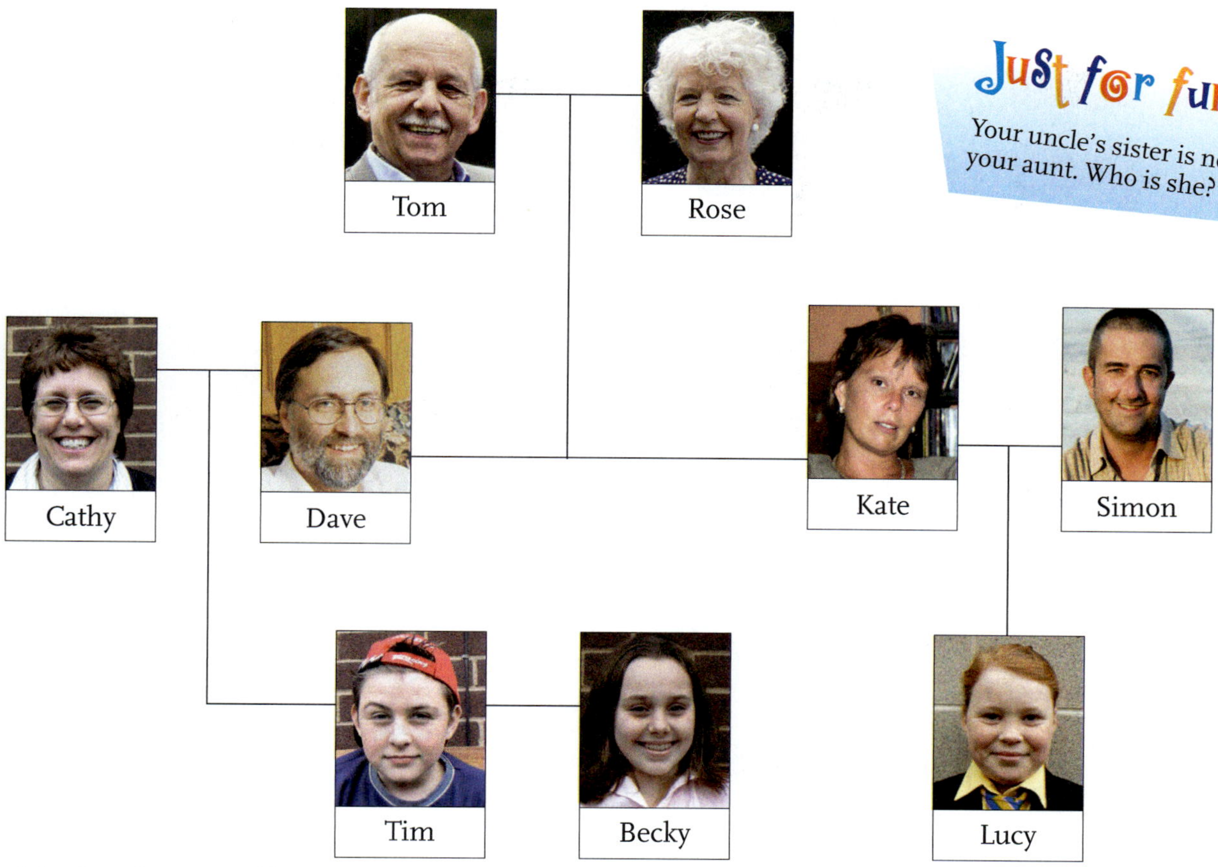

Just for fun
Your uncle's sister is not your aunt. Who is she?[1]

a) *Look at the Baxters' family tree. Who's who? Is it a), b) or c)? Sometimes two are correct.*

1 Tom is	a) Simon's brother.	b) Dave's uncle.	c) Lucy's grandfather. (circled)
2 Tim is	a) Becky's cousin.	b) Dave and Cathy's son.	c) Lucy's brother.
3 Lucy is	a) Tim and Becky's cousin.	b) Cathy's aunt.	c) Kate and Simon's daughter.
4 Cathy is	a) Lucy's aunt.	b) Tim and Becky's mother.	c) Lucy's mother.
5 Rose is	a) Tom's daughter.	b) Simon's aunt.	c) Dave and Kate's mother.

● ***b)*** *Now complete what Tim says about his family. Use* **'s** *or* **s'**.

Tim: This is the *Baxters'* family tree. Look. I'm Tim and my *sister's* name is Becky. My ______________ name is Kate and my ______________ name is Lucy. She's great. My ______________ names are Dave and Cathy. My ______________ names are Tom and Rose.

3116

[1] Your mother.

● 17 What's wrong? (Possessive form)

▸ p. 41 • GF 9 (p. 135)

Write the sentences again. Where is there an 's or an s'?

The Thompsons, Jo and Dan s grandparents, are at the Shaw s house. Dan and Jo s mum is the Thompson s daughter Catherine. Dan s favourite uncle is Catherine s brother Harry.
Dan and Jo have got three cousins too. Anne is Dan s favourite cousin and Mark is Jo s favourite cousin.

____

____

____

____

____

3217 ____

Just for fun

Ken's father is Rob's son, so Rob is Ken's ...[1]

18 Our pet photos (Possessive determiners)

▸ p. 41 • GF 8 (pp. 134–135)

Complete with: ***my, your, his, her, its, our, your, their***

1 *Jack* Look. That's me with ______ parrot. ______ name is Polly.

2 *Sophie* We've got a hamster. Look. Here it is in ______ cage.

3 *Toby* And here's a photo of ______ rabbits, Hip and Hop.
They are in ______ hutch.

Sophie This is Toby with ______ favourite rabbit, Hip.

4 *Jo* Here we are with Bill and Ben.

Ananda Oh! They're ______ cats. Great! I like cats.

5 *Sophie* This is ______ cousin Emma with ______ tortoise.

3218 6 *Ananda* ______ cousin has got a tortoise? What's ______ name?

[1] ... grandfather.

19 READING Tim's Saturday ▸ p. 49

a) *Look at the pictures. Then read the texts. Match the texts to the pictures.*

1 ☐

2 ☐

3 ☐

4 ☐

A

Before bed, Tim listens to rap music in his room. Barnabas sits in his favourite place – on Tim's bed. Tim's mum doesn't like that – but she doesn't see. Barnabas watches TV. Then he sleeps again – his favourite activity.

____

B

Tim does tricks on his skateboard. Barnabas sits and watches the birds. He doesn't climb trees. That's lots of work – and Barnabas doesn't like work. At lunch time the friends don't go home. They eat sandwiches in the park.

____

C

Saturday is Tim's favourite day. He gets up at nine and has breakfast with the family. Barnabas has breakfast too – a really big breakfast. He likes lots of cat food – but he thinks the Baxters don't give him enough.

____

D

Tim goes to the park and meets his friends there. Barnabas goes too, but he doesn't like sport. He likes an easy life, so Tim pulls him on his skateboard. Tim's friends laugh, and Barnabas is happy.

____

b) *What goes together? Match and write under the correct text in a).*

- A great place for a good time
- Lunch in the park
- Breakfast with the family
- The end of the day

3319

20 My dream house ▸ p. 50–51

a) *Read and choose words for your text. Mark your words with a felt tip.*

My dream house is a/an  old / new / big / little  flat. / house. / houseboat. / treehouse.

It's in  Germany. / England. / Australia. / New Zealand. / India. It has got a  park / garden and there are lots of  trees. / birds. / rabbits. / horses. / parrots.

My dream house has got  lots of / twelve / six / three / … rooms.

 Upstairs / Downstairs there's a/ there are  living room(s). / kitchen(s). / bedroom(s). / bathroom(s). / dining room(s).

b) *Use the text and words in a) and write about your dream house.*

My dream house is ______________________________

____

____

3420 ______________________________

c) *Now write about the things in the rooms. Choose from the box.*

there's a/an there are lots of/ two/ten/…	nice/big/great old/… red/blue/green/ orange/…	armchair • dishwasher • desk • bed • TV • lamp • wardrobe • posters • chairs • table • bath • sofa • fridge • cooker • sink • shower • computer • pictures • shelves

In the kitchen there's a ______________________________

____

In the bathroom there ______________________________

____

In my bedroom there ______________________________

____

1 What are they? Label the pets.

1 ________

4 ________

2 ________

5 ________

3 ________

6 ________

2 *'s* or *s'* ?

1 The (Kapoors) ________ flat is over the shop.

2 7PK is (Mr Kingsley) ________ form.

3 Bill and Ben are (Dan and Jo) ________ pets.

4 Barnabas is (Tim) ________ cat.

3 *His*, *her*, *its* or *their*?

1 The Carter-Browns and all ________ pets are at home today.

2 Prunella is at home. Sophie's room is ________ room too.

3 Jack is in the park with ________ dad.

4 Sophie's cousin Emma has got a tortoise. What's ________ name?

4 Complete the sentences with: *like*, *likes* (✓), *doesn't like*, *don't like* (✗)

	horses	fish	cats
Lucy	✓	✓	✗
Jo	✓	✗	✓
Tim	✓	✗	✓
Florian	✓	✗	✗
Becky	✓	✓	✓

1 Lucy ________ horses and fish. She ________ cats.

2 Jo and Tim ________ fish, but they ________ horses and cats.

3 Florian ________ fish or cats.

4 Becky ________ all the pets.

20 points

Now you

Write about pets: I've got a ... My friend/cousin/grandma has got a ... His/Her name is ... I like/I don't like ...

____

____

____

____

3505
3506
3507

Sports and hobbies

1 WORDS Sports and hobbies ► pp. 52–53

Write lists of Form 7PK's sports and hobbies.

play football | play computer games | go swimming | collect stamps
play hockey | make models | go riding | play the guitar

Sports

The students ...

play football

______

______

______

Hobbies

The students ...

play computer games

______

______

______

3601

2 REVISION Sophie goes riding ... (Simple present: statements) ► p. 53 • GF 7 (p. 132–134)

Complete the sentences. Use the words in exercise 1.

Sophie	√					x
Ananda	x			√		
Dan and Jo	x	x	√	√		
Jack		x	√		x	√

1 Sophie *goes* riding, but she *doesn't make* models.

2 Ananda ______ swimming, but she ______ riding.

3 Jack ______ models, but he ______ the guitar.

4 Dan and Jo ______ swimming, but they ______ riding.

3602 *5* Dan, Jo and Jack ______ computer games, but they ______ stamps.

Now you

Write about your sports and hobbies.

I ______

______, but I ______.

3 WORDS A picture puzzle ► p. 54

a) *Complete the picture puzzle.*

► 1										
2										
3										
4										
5										
6										
7						–				

3703

b) *Now complete the sentences about Florian with words from a).*

Florian plays in a football team. Look, he's got a red and white ______ and red ______.

His football ______ are black and white and his ______ are white.

4 Do you play ...? (Simple present: questions and short answers) ► p. 54 • GF 10a–b (p. 136)

Write questions. Then write short answers: ***Yes, I do. / No, I don't.***

1 Do you *play football*?
______

2 Do you ______?
______

3 Do ______?
______

4 ______
______

5 ______
______

5 Weekends (Simple present: questions) ▸ p. 54 • GF 10a (p. 136)

Write questions with words from the pink and blue boxes. Then tick (√) the yellow boxes.

read • listen • *go* • play • meet

1 ... to the shops?
2 ... to music?
3 ... the guitar?
4 ... your friends?
5 ... comics in bed?

Weekends	🙂	☹
Do you *go to the shops*?		
Do you ______________________?		
Do ______________________?		
______________________		
______________________		

6 Ananda's hockey shoes (Simple present: questions and short answers) ▸ p. 54 • GF 10a–b (p. 136)

Complete the questions with do or does. Then write answers: Yes, she does. / No, they don't. / ...

1 *Does* Ananda need hockey shoes? Yes, *she does.*
2 *Do* Ananda and her mum need a shop assistant? Yes, ______________.
3 ______ size four fit? Yes, ______________.
4 ______ Ananda like the colour? No, ______________.
5 ______ she try on red and white shoes? Yes, ______________.
3806 6 ______ Ananda and her mum take T-shirts too? No, ______________.

7 Free time (Simple present: questions) ▸ p. 54 • GF 10a (p. 136)

Write questions.

1 Jo likes sport. (And Jack?)
Does Jack like sport?

2 Prunella collects plates. (And Sophie?)
____

3 Ananda and Sophie go swimming. (And Dan and Jo?)
____

4 Ananda plays hockey. (And Prunella?)
____

5 Jack makes models. (And Dan and Jo?)
____

8 What does Ananda ask? (Simple present: wh-questions)

► p. 55 • GF 10c (p. 137)

Complete her questions with: **What**, **When**, **Who**, **Where**

Rhyme time

I've got two hamsters,
Kim and Kay,
They've got a big cage
With lots of hay[1].
They play all night and sleep all day –
But because they're hamsters,
That's OK.

Ananda's questions:		Sophie's answers:
1	*What* do Hip and Hop eat?	Lots of carrots.
2	_______ do they play?	In the garden.
3	_______ do they sleep?	At night.
4	_______ do they drink?	Just water.
5	_______ cleans the hutch?	Toby and I.

9 STUDY SKILLS Wörter nachschlagen

► p. 55 • SF 4 (p. 122)

a) *The boxes are full of Sophie's old things. Write the words in alphabetical order.*

photos • books • posters • boxes • pictures • packets of stamps • CDs • calendars • *balls* • *comics* • birthday cards • computer games

Just for fun

Where does Thursday come before Wednesday?[2]

b) *Add the following words to the list of p-words in a):* **pens**, **pencils**, **poems**. *Where do they go? Check with the Dictionary (pp. 179–191).*

packets of stamps, _______________

____

3909

[1] hay [heɪ] *Heu* [2] In the dictionary.

10 PRONUNCIATION [æ] and [eɪ] ▸ p. 56 5

*Listen to the words. Where are the [æ]-sounds, like **cat**? Where are the [eɪ]-sounds, like **snake**? Colour the **cat**-words **red** and the **snake**-words **blue**.*

4010

cat	snake	flat
bag	plate	day
late	rabbit	black
make	back	table
stamp	act	plan
say	lamp	place

11 Sentence snakes (Adverbs: word order) ▸ p. 56 • GF 11 (p. 137)

Cross out the wrong word. Colour the correct word. Then write the sentence.

1

We always get up early.

2

3

4

5

6

12 About Tim (Adverbs: word order) ▸ p. 56 • GF 11 (p. 137)

Write sentences about Tim.

Does he …?	always	usually	often	sometimes	never
1 help at home?				√	
2 make breakfast?				√	
3 go to football matches?	√				
4 get up before 7 o'clock?					√
5 watch TV after school?		√			
6 go to bed late?			√		

1 Tim *sometimes helps at home.*

2 He ______________________________.

3 ______________________________

4 ______________________________

5 ______________________________

4112 *6* ______________________________

Now you

How often do you do the things in exercise 12? Write sentences with: ***always, usually, often, sometimes, never***

I ______________________________

____

____

____

____

Just for fun

A: I often play computer games with my dog.
B: Wow! You've got a very clever pet.
A: Not really. I usually win.

____

____

____

13 WORDS *Go*, *play* or *do*? ▸ p. 57

a) *Match, then write.*

badminton · swimming · hockey · judo · yoga · tennis · basketball · dancing · riding

go · play · do

go swimming, ______________________________

play ______________________________

do ______________________________

b) *Now complete Toby's sentences with the correct form of* ***go***, ***play*** *or* ***do***.

Do you ____________ football or basketball? In our family we all like sport. I ____________ judo. Emily ____________ tennis. Sophie likes horses, so she ____________ riding. In summer we all ____________ swimming. Mum ____________ yoga – and my dad watches sport on TV.

4213

14 WORDS Opposites[1] ▸ p. 57

a) *Which words go together? Find, colour and write opposites.*

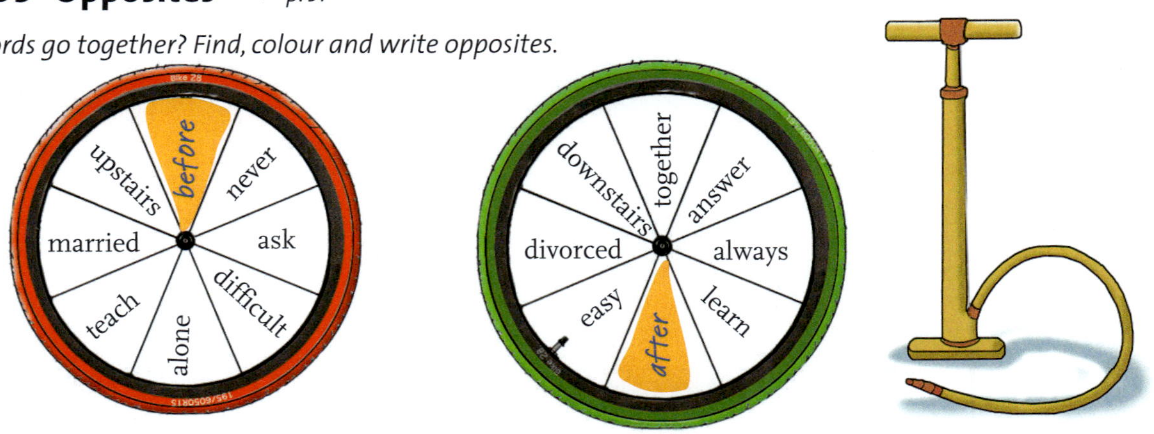

before – after

______________ – ______________

______________ – ______________

______________ – ______________

______________ – ______________

______________ – ______________

______________ – ______________

______________ – ______________

b) *Complete with words from a).*

Prunella ____________ plays tennis with Uncle Henry. He ____________ wins because he hasn't got a head. He likes the old house, but it looks different ____________ 100 years. Sophie and Prunella's room is ____________. ____________, in the living room, there's a piano. Prunella can play. It's ____________ with a head, but it's ____________ for poor Uncle Henry.

[1] opposite ['ɒpəzɪt] *Gegenteil*

15 Who has to do what? (have to/has to) ▸ *p. 57 • GF 12 (p. 138)*

*Write sentences with **have to**, **has to**, **don't have to** or **doesn't have to**. Choose from the box.*

> *do his Maths homework* • go to her piano lesson • clean his bike • get up early • make his bed • clean the kitchen

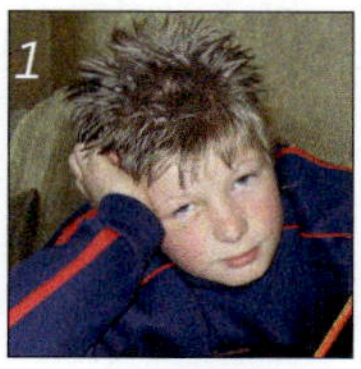

1 Florian

4 Becky

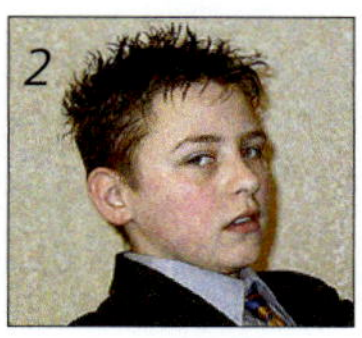

2 Tim

5 Tim and Becky

3 Becky and Tim

6 Florian

1 *Florian has to do his Maths homework.*

2 ______________________________

3 ______________________________

4 ______________________________

5 ______________________________

4315 6 ______________________________

Now you

What do you have to do every day? Write two sentences.

____

____

What don't you have to do every day? Write two sentences.

____

____

16 WORKING WITH THE TEXT The SHoCK Team ▸ pp. 65–66

***a)** Read pp. 65–66 in your student's book again. Match the text to the pictures. Write the letters A–F in the boxes.*

1 

2 

3 

4 

5 

6 

A He sees a scary man in black outside Mr Green's room.

B Jack is alone in his room.

C The man runs outside. Jack can't see him on the street.

D Suddenly there's a noise, so he looks downstairs.

E They say he has to tell the police or his parents.

F Jack tells his friends about the scary man in black.

***b)** Who thinks what? Match the bubbles to the friends in the SHoCK Team.*

I've got an idea. I need a piece of paper.

I've got a piece of paper. Here it is.

Jack has to tell his parents about the man in black.

We all have to watch Mr Green.

Yes! 'Detective Jo Shaw'…

Jack has to phone the police.

Ananda

Sophie

Jack

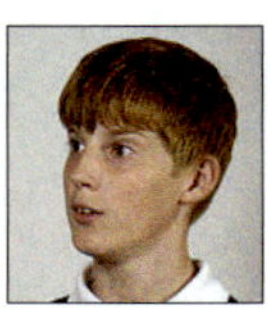
Dan

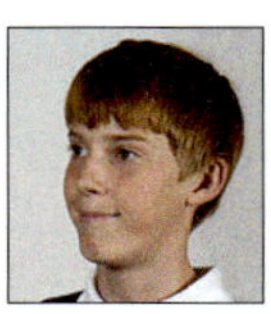
Jo

***c)** Write answers.*

1 Does the man in black go into Mr Green's room?

____

2 What does Jack think about Mr Green?

____

3 What do the children have to do?

____

***d)** In the History lesson, Jack writes a code message[1] to the SHoCK Team. What does it say?*

1	2	3	4	5	6	7	8	9	10	11	12	13	14	15	16	17	18	19	20	21	22	23	24	25	26
A	B	C	D	E	F	G	H	I	J	K	L	M	N	O	P	Q	R	S	T	U	V	W	X	Y	Z

23 8 5 18 5   4 15 5 19   13 18   7 18 5 5 14   7 15   1 6 20 5 18

_ _ _ _ _   _ _ _ _   _ _   _ _ _ _ _   _ _   _ _ _ _ _

2 18 5 1 11 6 1 19 20?   23 5   8 1 22 5   20 15   6 9 14 4   15 21 20!

_ _ _ _ _ _ _ _ _ ?   _ _   _ _ _ _   _ _   _ _ _ _   _ _ _ !

[1] code message [kəʊd 'mesɪdʒ] *verschlüsselte Nachricht*

Activity page 1

Word pairs ▸ Welcome · Unit 1 · Topic 1

- *Cut out the parts.*
- *Put the pairs together.*
- *What have you got?*

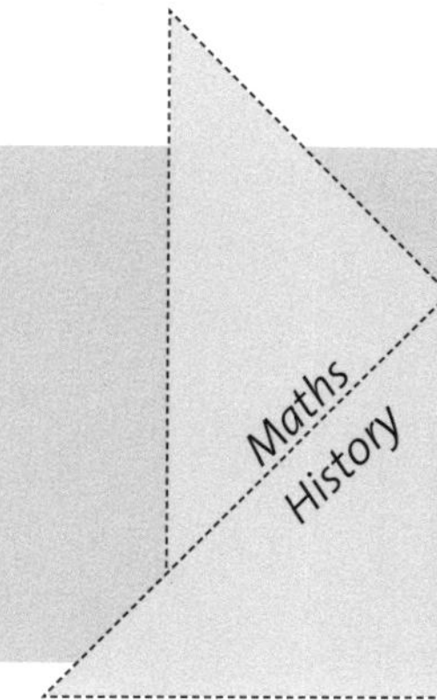

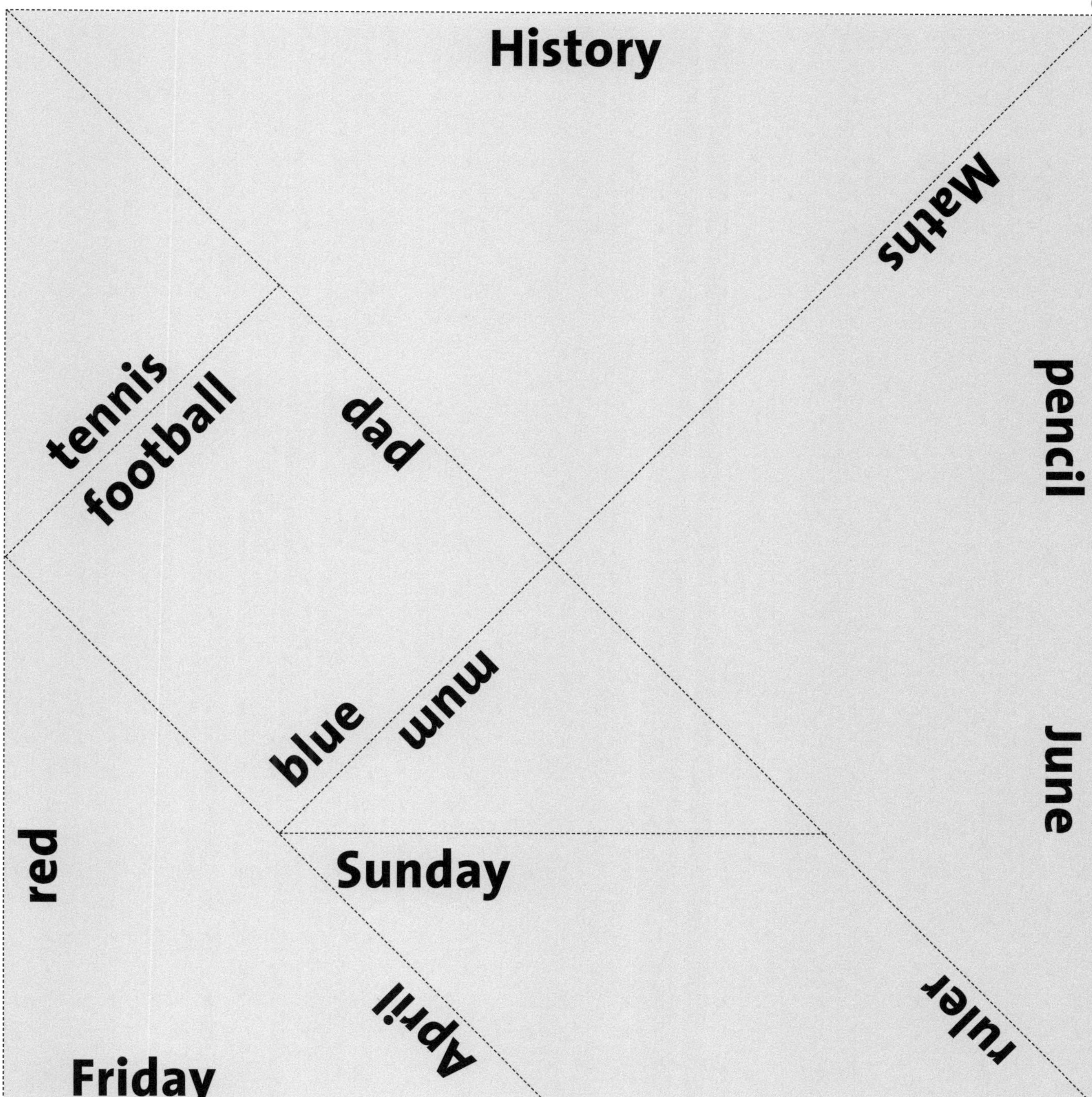

Activity page 2

British money ▸ Topic 3 *(p. 67)*

- *Cut out the money.*
- *Glue the correct parts.*
- *How much money is there?*
- *You can act with this money in your jumble sale.*

Activity page 3

Food memory game

▸ Unit 4

- *Cut out the word cards and the pictures.*
- *Put the cards on the table, so that you can't see the words and the pictures.*
- *Take two cards and match the correct picture and the word card. Go on!*
- *You can play this game with a partner.*

	**a birthday cake**		**a plate of cheese**	
ice cream		**potatoes**		**sausages**
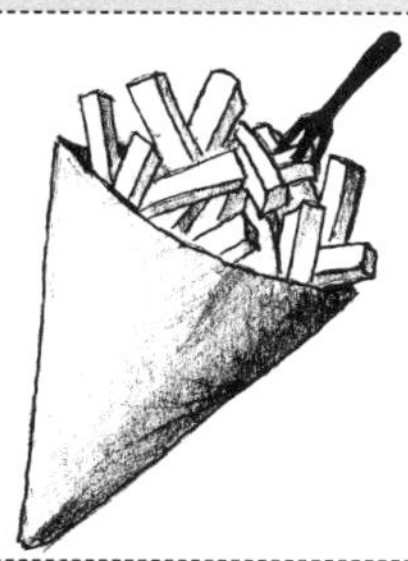	**a piece of cake**		**a jug of milk**	
a bowl of salad		**a glass of orange juice**		**a packet of crisps**
	**chips**		**chicken**	
sweets		**sandwiches**		**a bottle of cola**

Activity page 4

A Christmas card

▸ Topic 6 *(p. 113)*

- *Cut out the Christmas card and cut out the three sides of the little window.*
- *Cut out the picture of the sock. Put glue on the sides.*
- *Glue the picture of the sock in the window.*
- *Cut out Merry Christmas. Put the two words at the top of the card.*
- *Colour the card.*

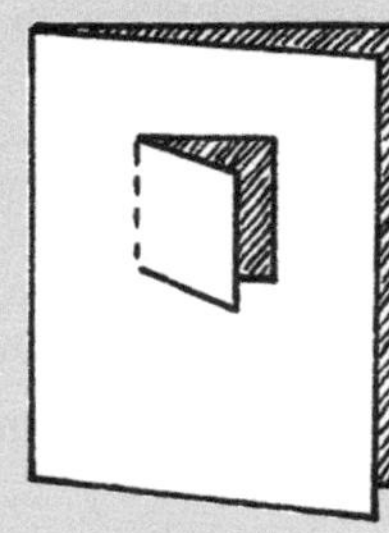

17 In the Oxfam shop ▸ p. 67

○ ***a)*** *How much is it? Write the prices on the things in the Oxfam shop.*

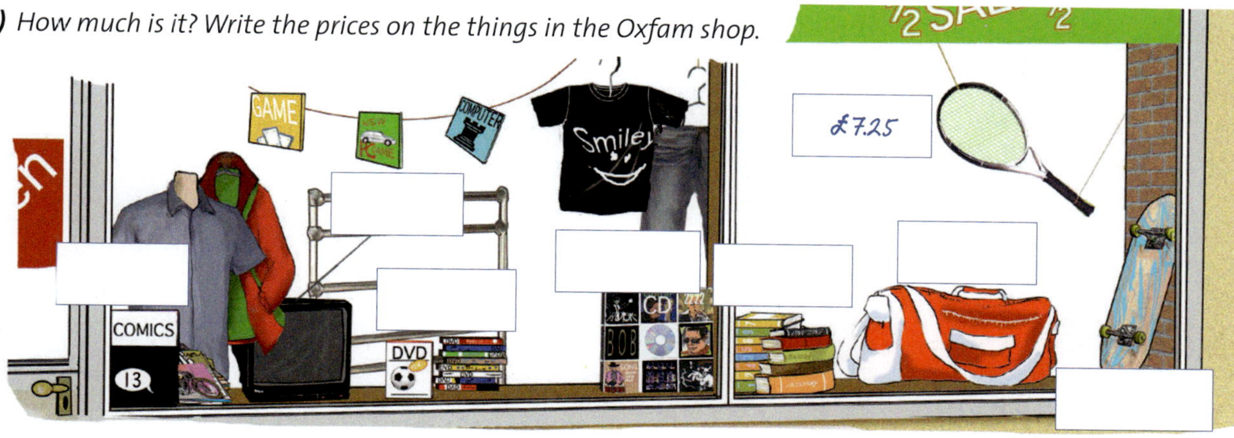

The tennis racket is seven pounds twenty-five.
The bag is six pounds fifty.
4517 The CDs are two pounds eighty-five each[1].
The comics are seventy p each.
The computer games are five pounds each.
The DVDs are three pounds forty-nine each.
The skateboard is ten pounds ninety-nine.
The books are two pounds sixty each.

b) *Jo is in the Oxfam shop. What does Jo say? Write* J*. What does the shop assistant say? Write* A*. Then write correct sentences in the speech bubbles.*

___ Oh, then I'll take it. Here's the money.
A Hello. Can I help you?
___ Let's see. It's £10.99.
___ And here's your change. Thank you.
___ Oh, that's too much.
How much is the bag?
___ Mmm. I've only got £6.50 and 25p is for the bus.
___ The bag is £6.50.
J Yes, how much is the skateboard, please?
___ Mmm. Well, I can take 25p off.
___ Thank you. Bye.

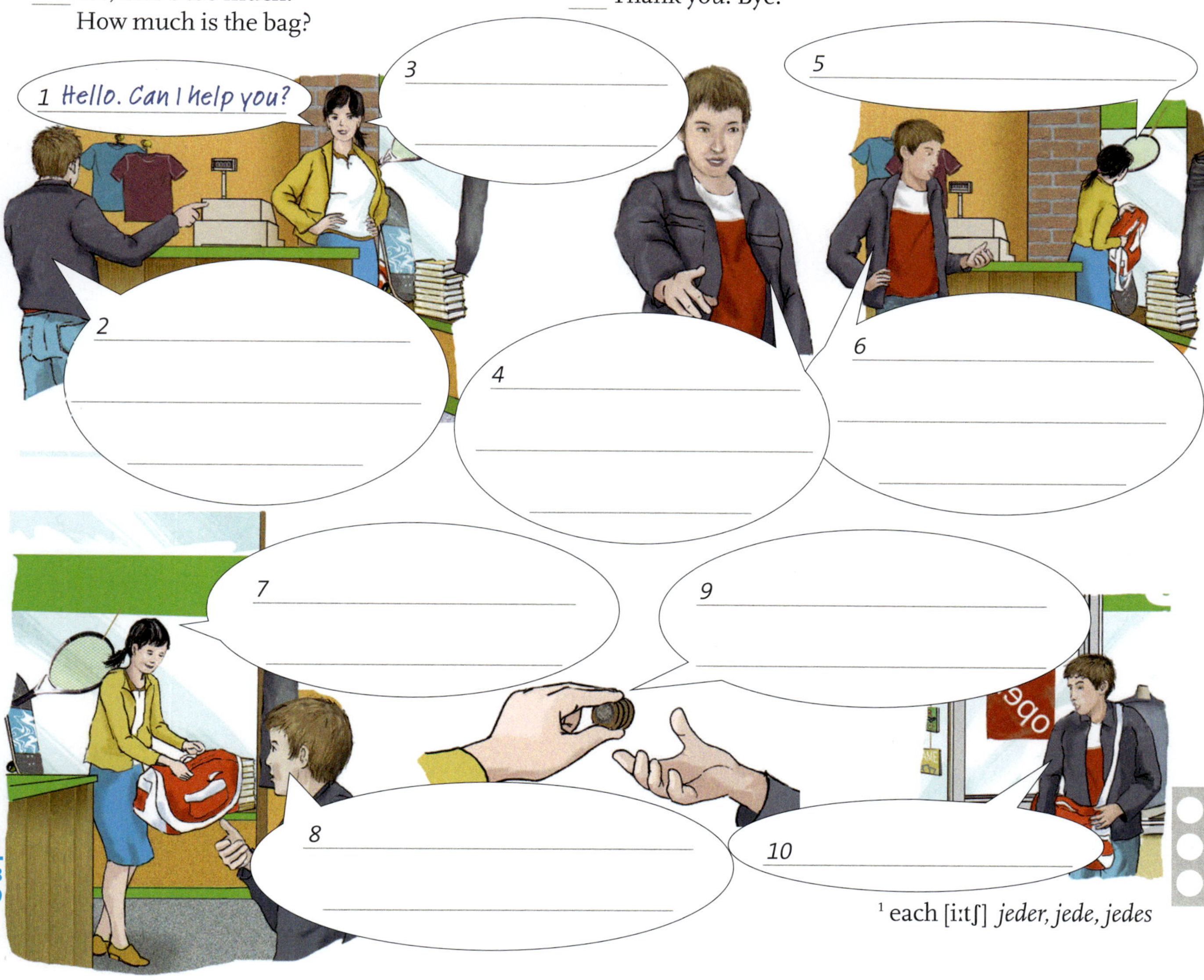

4518
4519

[1] each [iːtʃ] *jeder, jede, jedes*

1 Sports and hobbies

Use collect, go, make, play and complete the sentences.

1 Jack ____________________.

2 Sophie ____________________.

3 Dilip ____________________.

4 Ananda ____________________.

4

1

3

2

2 Ask about the people in ( ).

1 Jo and Jack like music. (Dan and Sophie?) ____________________

2 Prunella plays tennis. (Sophie?) ____________________

3 Ananda writes e-mails. (you?) ____________________

4 Jack's mum does yoga. (Jack's dad?) ____________________

3 Make correct sentences.

1 goes/never/Jay/to football matches ____________________

2 write/I/don't/often/e-mails ____________________

3 Becky/play/does/basketball ? ____________________

4 does/Prunella/tennis/play/where ? ____________________

4 Write what they *have to* do or *don't have to* do.

1 At school we ____________________ listen to the teacher.

2 Most days Jack ____________________ help at the B&B.

3 In the holidays we ____________________ get up early.

4 Prunella ____________________ go to school.

16 points

● Now you

Write four sentences about sports and hobbies. Do you play football or tennis? Do you collect or make things? What about your friends and family?

____

____

____

4605
4606

Jetzt kann ich ...

	Sehr gut!	OK	Verbessern!
HÖREN: Ich kann ...			
... die Arbeitsanweisungen und Fragen im Unterricht verstehen.	☐	☐	☐
... Fragen über mich, meine Familie, Haustiere und Freizeit verstehen.	☐	☐	☐
... die Hörtexte der Units 1–3 verstehen.	☐	☐	☐
SPRECHEN: Ich kann ...			
... jemanden begrüßen, mich vorstellen und mich verabschieden.	☐	☐	☐
... jemanden nach dem Alter fragen und fragen, woher er/sie kommt.	☐	☐	☐
... über mich, meine Freunde, Familie und Freizeit sprechen.	☐	☐	☐
... über Haustiere und ihre Behausungen sprechen.	☐	☐	☐
... ein einfaches Einkaufsgespräch führen.	☐	☐	☐
... die Wörter der Units 1–3 richtig aussprechen.	☐	☐	☐
LESEN: Ich kann ...			
... die Arbeitsanweisungen in meinem Buch/Workbook verstehen.	☐	☐	☐
... die Texte und Dialoge der Units 1–3 lesen und verstehen.	☐	☐	☐
SCHREIBEN: Ich kann ...			
... Wörter und kurze Sätze richtig abschreiben.	☐	☐	☐
... über mich, meine Freunde, Familie, Haustiere und Freizeit schreiben.	☐	☐	☐
... über unsere Wohnung/unser Haus/verschiedene Zimmer schreiben.	☐	☐	☐
... über meinen Tagesablauf schreiben.	☐	☐	☐
... Wörter für Familienmitglieder und Verwandte richtig schreiben.	☐	☐	☐
... schreiben, wem etwas gehört. Dazu verwende ich *'s* oder *s'*.	☐	☐	☐
LAND UND LEUTE: Ich weiß ...			
..., wie der Schultag britischer Schülerinnen und Schüler aussieht.	☐	☐	☐
..., wie britische Schülerinnen und Schüler ihre Freizeit verbringen.	☐	☐	☐
LERNEN UND ARBEITEN: Ich kann ...			
... in meinem Buch Vokabeln und Grammatikregeln nachschlagen.	☐	☐	☐
... mithilfe von Vorgaben ein Vokabelnetzwerk oder eine Mindmap ergänzen.	☐	☐	☐
... mit meiner Lieblingsmethode Vokabeln selbstständig lernen.	☐	☐	☐
... mit einem Partner oder einer Partnerin und in einer Gruppe arbeiten.	☐	☐	☐

WIE ICH MICH VERBESSERN KÖNNTE: Ich könnte ...

- ... meinen Karteikasten häufiger benutzen. ☐
- ... Texte aus meinem Buch zu Hause laut lesen. ☐
- ... Texte aus meinem Buch auswendig lernen. ☐
- ... schwierige Wörter häufiger abschreiben. ☐
- ... kurze Texte abschreiben. ☐
- ... Dialoge mit Freunden üben. ☐

Unit 4 Party, party!

1 WORDS Sophie's shopping list ▸ pp. 68–69

a) *Write Sophie's shopping list of food and drinks for the party.*

chocolate cake • carrots • cheese • chicken • chips • biscuits • cola • crisps • fruit • ice cream • lemonade • orange juice • sausages • sweets

1 
2 
3 
4 
5 
6 
7 
8 
9 
10 
11 
12 
13 
14 

Shopping list

1 ______	8 ______
2 ______	9 ______
3 ______	10 ______
4 ______	11 ______
5 ______	12 ______
6 ______	13 ______
7 ______	14 ______

b) *Draw and label your favourite party food. Choose three things.*

chicken • sausages • fruit salad • chocolate cake • ice cream • carrot salad • hamburgers

______	______	______

4801

Now you

What food and drinks do you like? What don't you like?

I like ______________________________.

I don't like ______________________________.

2 WORDS What's on the table? ▸ p. 69

Match words from the boxes. Write: a plate of ..., a bottle of ...

bowl • bottle • basket • plate • jug

cheese • fruit • milk • orange juice • cornflakes

1 a plate of cheese

2 ____________________

3 ____________________

4 ____________________

4902 5 ____________________

3 Would you like some tea? ▸ p. 69

Complete Becky's questions and Florian's answers.

1  2  3  4 

1 *Becky:* Would you like some tea? ____________________

2 *Florian:* No, thank you. But I ____________________.

3 *Becky:* And would ____________________?

4903 4 *Florian:* No, __________. But ____________________.

4 An invitation ▸ p. 70

Florian invites Becky and Tim to a barbecue. What does the invitation say? Look at p. 70 of your student's book again. Then complete the text.

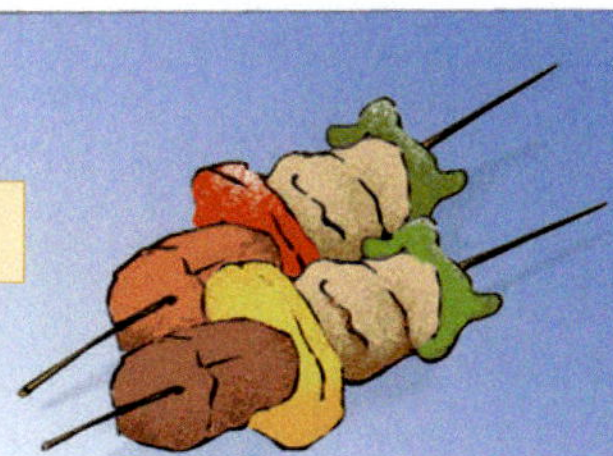

Florian's barbecue

__________ Becky and Tim

__________ come __________ my barbecue!

__________? At 24 Gordon Road

When? __________ Saturday, 16th April

Time? __________ 2.30

5 Sophie's party (Subject and object pronouns) ▸ pp. 70 • GF 13 (pp. 138–139)

○ ***a)*** *Match and colour.*

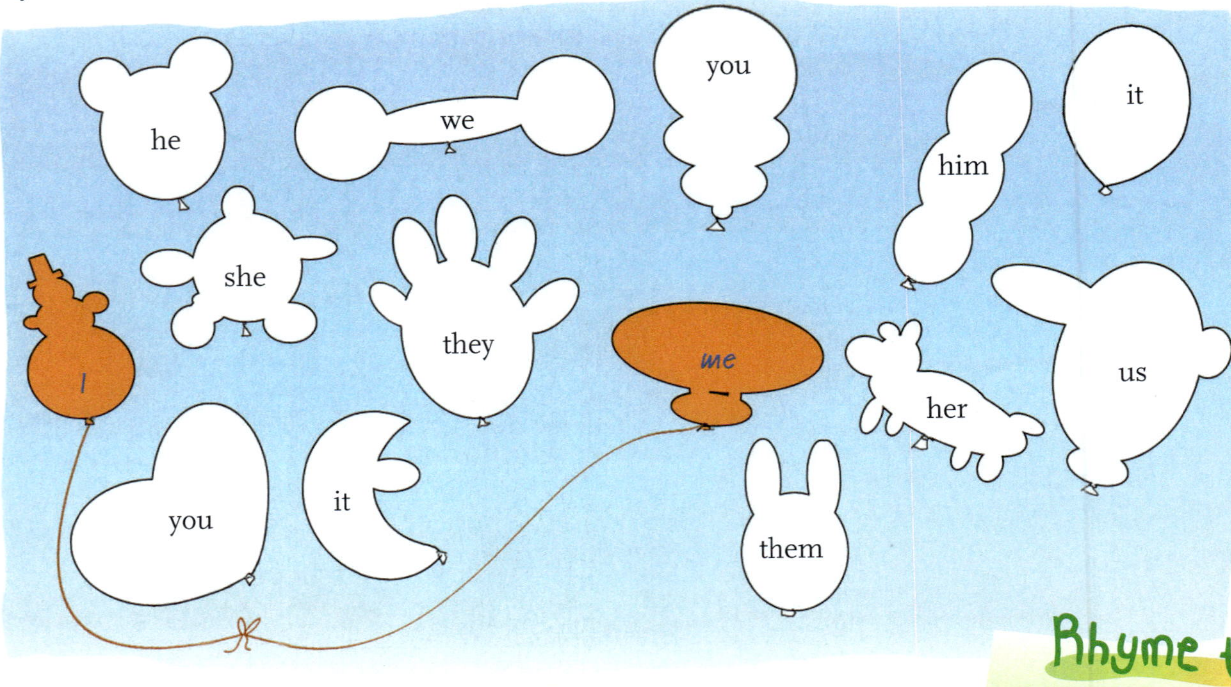

Rhyme time

Friends and invitations,
Cake and ice cream too.
I ♥ birthdays,
What about you?

b) *Now complete with:* ***me, you, him, her, it, us, them***

1 *Sophie* Birthday parties are great. I really like ________________.

2 *Prunella* Would you like a nice cake from ____________? We can make ____________ together.

3 *Sophie* Prunella, I really can't invite ________________ to my party. I'm sorry.

4 *Prunella* Well, Uncle Henry likes parties. Can you invite ________________? – No, you can't.

You can't invite ____________ because we aren't real people. Right?

5005

But Ananda can come. You like ________________ – and she's real.

● **6 Invitations** (Object pronouns for German '*sie*') ▸ p. 70 • GF 13 (pp. 138–139)

Find and circle the correct word.

1 *Sophie* Where's my invitation list, Prunella? I can't find (them/it/her).

2 *Prunella* Have Dan and Jo got an invitation? You like (her/them/it).

What about your cousin Emma? Have you got (it/her/them) on your list?

And what about all the neighbours' children?

3 *Sophie* No, I really can't invite (her/it/them). They make too much noise.

Prunella Right – and they eat too much.

Sophie Prunella!

7 STUDY SKILLS Notizen machen ► p. 71 • SF 5 (p. 123)

Mark the key words, then write them.
The SHoCK Team meets after school.

Jack OK, SHoCK Team detectives. We have to find out about Mr Green. Who can do what?

Sophie I can write down our ideas.

Jo We can follow him at weekends. I can start tomorrow. I can be at the B&B at 8.30. What about you, Dan?

Dan Yes, great, and what about some photos of Mr Green?

Ananda Maybe I can find out about bank robbers in the computer.

Jack Great idea! And I can follow Mr Green on my bike on Sunday.

Dan Then we can all meet on Sunday evening. OK?

Jack OK, let's meet in the park at six o'clock.

5107

SHoCK Team – Ideas
Find out about Mr Green

Jo – follow – weekends
– start tomorrow
– B&B – 8.30

Dan ______________________

Ananda ______________________

____

Jack ______________________

____

Dan ______________________

____

Jack ______________________

8 WORDS The mad computer ► p. 71

a) *The mad computer sometimes writes wrong letters. Write the words with the correct letters.*

?nv?t&t?#n ______
f%nny ______
∫xp∫ns?v∫ ______
b#r?ng ______
pr∫s∫nt ______
s%ngl&ss∫s ______
d?ff?c%lt ______

b) *Now put the correct words from a) in Ananda's e-mail to Jack.*

Hi, Jack!

I've got an ______________ to Sophie's party too. I've got an idea. Let's buy her a ______________ together – not too ______________ because I haven't got much money – maybe a ______________ present? It's ______________. Not just chocolate. That's ______________.

Have you got any ideas? What about some ______________? See you at school.

Ananda

9 Some sausages and some milk (some and any) ▸ p. 71 • GF 14 (p. 139)

Tim and Becky go shopping for their mum.

Shopping list
milk
cheese
sausages
crisps
ice cream
biscuits

a) *What have Tim and Becky got in their baskets? Use* **some**.

Becky has got some milk, some ____________________,

____________ and ____________.

Tim has got ____________, ____________

____________ and ____________.

b) *Which three things haven't they got? Use* **any**.

They haven't got ____________, ____________ or ____________.

10 Tim's birthday list (some and any) ▸ p. 71 • GF 14 (p. 139)

What does Tim want for his birthday? Look at the list. Use **some** *and* **any**.

✓ posters
✗ books
✓ CDs
✗ hockey shoes
✗ socks
✓ money
✓ chocolate
✓ other sweets

1 He wants some posters, but he doesn't want any books.

2 He wants ____________ CDs, but he doesn't want ____________.

3 He doesn't want ____________, but he wants ____________.

4 Does he want ____________ chocolate?

5 And does he want ____________? – Yes, he does.

5210

Now you

What do you want for your next birthday? Use **some** *and* **any**.

I want ____________,

but I don't want ____________.

11 At the Baxters' (Present progressive: positive statements) ▸ p. 72 • GF 15–16a (p. 140)

It's two o'clock on Sunday afternoon. What are the Baxters doing? Make sentences.

Barnabas Mrs Baxter Mr Baxter Grandma and Grandpa Tim and Florian Becky and Lucy	is are	tidying sleeping cleaning watching playing making	the living room. a computer game. a mess. TV. the cooker. on the sofa.

1 Barnabas is sleeping on the sofa.

2 Mrs Baxter is cleaning ______.

3 ______

4 ______

5 ______

5311 6 ______

12 Where are the verbs? (-ing-forms) ▸ p. 72 • GF 16a (p. 140)

○ ***a)*** *Find and write nine verbs.*

F	E	E	D	K	S	T
O	S	R	U	N	J	A
L	W	R	I	T	E	K
L	I	Y	G	I	V	E
O	M	K	E	G	E	T
W	A	L	K	K	I	L

feed ______ ______
______ ______
______ ______
______ ______
______

b) *Now write the verbs in the correct list.*

+ ing	e̸ + ing	double letter + ing
feed – feeding	take – taking	swim – swimming

13 Becky's dream birthday (Present progressive: positive statements) ▸ p. 72 • GF 16a (p. 140)

Becky is thinking about her dream birthday. What's happening? Choose verbs from the box.

dance • drink • eat • give • ~~have~~ • play • sing • sit • swim • talk

I'*m having* a big barbecue at my dream house.

We ____________ chicken and hamburgers and we ____________ banana juice. All my friends ____________ me lots of presents.

My favourite band ____________ really great music.

Now I ____________ with my favourite pop star.

Tim ____________ at the swimming pool[1]. He ____________ to some Hollywood stars. Some of the guests ____________ in the pool. Now my favourite film stars ____________ 'Happy birthday to Becky'... It's my dream party!

5413

14 Prunella's visitor (Present progressive: positive and negative statements) ▸ p. 72 • GF 16a (p. 140)

Prunella has got a visitor. It's Uncle Henry. What are they doing in the pictures?
Write two sentences for each picture.

1 It's 2.30.
Is Prunella making sandwiches or is she making tea?
She isn't making tea. She's making sandwiches.

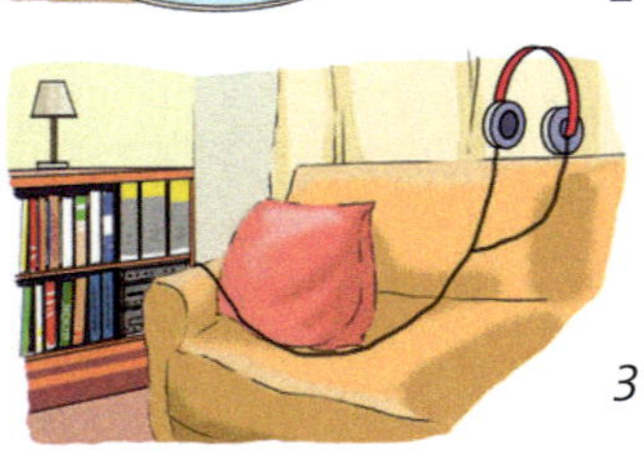

2 It's 3 o'clock.
Is Uncle Henry listening to music or is he watching TV?

____

3 It's 3.15.
Are they reading newspapers or are they looking at old photos?

____

____

4 It's 3.30.
Is Prunella playing the piano or is she dancing?

____

5 Now it's 4 o'clock.
Are they eating ice cream or are they having sandwiches and tea?

____

____

[1] swimming pool ['swɪmɪŋ puːl] *Schwimmbecken*

15 Questions and answers (Present progressive: questions and short answers)

▸ p. 74 • GF 16b (p. 141)

*Write questions. Then look at exercise **14** and write short answers:* **Yes, she is. / No, …**

1 

Uncle Henry/newspapers/reading/is ?

____

2 

having/sandwiches and tea/are/Prunella and Uncle Henry ?

____

____

3 

Prunella/playing/is/the piano?

____

Just for fun

A: What are you doing?
B: I'm eating this cake.
A: But that's **my** cake.
B: OK. Then I'm eating **your** cake.

Now you

What are you and your family doing now? Write in your exercise book:
My mum/dad/sister/brother/ … is/are doing/…

16 PRONUNCIATION [əʊ] or [ɒ]?

▸ p. 74 🎧 6

Which words are like phone *[əʊ] and which are like* sock *[ɒ]? Listen to the words and match.*

5516

phone [əʊ]

poster, clock, hockey, home, bottle, old, hobby, yoga, bowl, comic, boat, alone, box

sock [ɒ]

17 WORDS Where are the body words?

a) *Find and write the body words.*

s	x	f	h	e	a	d	y	z	p
h	a	i	r	e	y	e	l	e	g
o	a	n	a	u	o	h	a	n	d
u	d	g	r	b	x	z	i	j	n
l	f	e	m	m	o	u	t	h	o
d	a	r	f	o	o	t	o	y	s
e	c	s	e	k	n	e	e	t	e
r	e	o	e	b	d	a	s	m	o
p	c	t	t	e	d	r	m	v	r

▶	▼
head	shoulder
______	______
______	______
______	______
______	______
______	______
______	______
______	

18 READING Tim's party ▸ p. 82

a) *Read about Tim's birthday party. Write the names of his friends in the picture.*

It's Tim's 12th birthday. Look, he's having a disco with all his friends. Lots of his classmates are here. I'm here too – but Tim doesn't know that. I haven't got an invitation, so I'm hiding ... Can you see me? The party room is great. There's a table with presents – and lots of food. There isn't any cat food, but there's some chicken, some fish, some sausages ...

The party guests are all having a good time. What are they doing? Well, a DJ is playing the music. His name is Tony. Tim is talking to him. Pat and Jill are looking at the presents. Pat is the girl with long hair. Sue is dancing with Florian. She's wearing jeans and a nice red T-shirt – my favourite colour. Ed and Alex are eating sandwiches. Ed is drinking lemonade too. Ali is telling funny jokes and Gina is laughing. Lucy has got her guitar with her. Great – she isn't playing it. She's bad, but the DJ's music is cool. Mmm. They aren't looking. Yes, now is a good time ...

Twenty minutes later ...

Ed Where's the fish? The plate is empty.
Ali There isn't any chicken. Where is it all?
Sue And who's got all the sausages?

b) *Now complete the sentences.*

1 Tim is having a disco because it's ______________________.

2 Barnabas hasn't got an invitation, so ______________________.

3 In the party room there's a big table with ______________________.

4 Sue is wearing ______________________.

5 Gina is laughing because Ali ______________________.

6 Lucy has got her guitar with her, but she ______________________.

5618 *7* Barnabas eats all the ______________________.

1 What does Mrs Carter-Brown need from the shops?

Write her shopping list.

1 ________________

2 ________________

3 ________________

4 ________________

5 ________________

6 ________________

2 Complete with: *me*, *him*, *her*, *it*, *them*

1 *Tim* Where's Mum's shopping list? I can't find ________.

2 *Becky* I don't know. Don't ask ________.

3 *Tim* Well, where's Mum? Let's ask ________.

4 *Becky* Where are Mum and Dad? I can't see ________.

5 *Tim* Dad is in the garden. Let's ask ________.

3 What's in the fridge? *Some* or *any*?

1 *Tim* There's ________ fruit, but there aren't ________ carrots.

2 *Becky* And is there ________ milk?

3 *Tim* No, but there's ________ lemonade.

4 What*'s happening* at the station? Use: *call*, *get on*, *give*, *read*, *run*

1 A man ________________ a newspaper.

2 Two girls ________________ the train.

3 A boy ________________ somebody on his mobile.

4 A woman ________________ a girl some money.

5 Two boys ________________ to the train.

20 points

Now you

5705
5706

Think about your dream birthday party. What are you and your party guests doing? What's happening? For ideas look at exercises 13 (p. 54) and 18 (p. 56). Write a short text (about six sentences) in your exercise book.

Unit 5 School: not just lessons

1 WORDS Happy birthday, Grandpa

▸ pp. 84–85

Oh no! Which words can't Jo's grandpa read? Write the words.

Choir • Computer • paint • pirates • practise • programmes • rehearsal • results • ship • *Spring*

Happy birthday, Grandpa!

It's our … Show next week. We have to p… a lot. I sing in the Junior …ir. My favourite song is about … . My friend Ananda is in the C…p…r Club. They're making the p…ra…s. Dan can …t so he's in the Art Club. They're painting a … for our pirate scene. We're all nervous. It's the last … on Tuesday. Sport is great too. Our Year 7 football …u… are always good. That's all for now. Have a great birthday!

Jo – and Ben … Sorry!!

Spring, ______

______

______

______

______

______

______

2 WORDS School notice board

▸ pp. 84–85

The names of the clubs are wrong. Write the correct names. Then find the missing club.

1 **Dance Club**
Can you act in plays? We meet on Fridays after school, Room 10

2 **Junior Band**
Great result! Last match Portway 1 Cotham 3

3 **Drama Club**
Do you play the guitar or the clarinet? We meet on Mondays after school, Room 17

4 **Junior Choir**
Do you like dancing? Come to our club on Wednesday at 4 pm, Room 20

5 **Football Team**
Can you sing? Come and sing with us. Thursdays, Room 17

6 ....
Can you paint pictures? We meet on Tuesdays after school, Room 11

1 *Drama Club*

2 ______

3 ______

4 ______

5 ______

6 ______

5802
5803

3 An e-mail from Becky (was/were in positive statements) ▸ p. 86 • GF 17–18 (p. 141)

Here is an e-mail from Becky to her friend Lisa. Fill in **was** *or* **were**.

Hi, Lisa!

Last weekend I *was* at a party. My classmates *were* there too. The food ________ really great – so we ________ all very happy. There ________ some good salads and pizza. The music ________ fantastic (lots of noise!) – but the neighbours ________ OK because their children ________ at the party too.

________ you at a party last weekend? ________ it a birthday party? Tell me about it!

Becky

4 Where were Tim's things? (was/were in positive and negative statements) ▸ p. 86 • GF 17–18 (p. 141)

Tim's room looks nice today. But where were his things last Friday?
Write sentences about Tim's things with **was**, **wasn't**, **were** *and* **weren't**.
Write about:
1 his shoes 2 his football 3 his comics 4 his clock 5 his school things

Tim's room today

Tim's room last Friday

1 *His shoes weren't* in the wardrobe. *They were* on the chair.

2 ________ on the wardrobe. ________ on the bed.

3 ________ on the shelf. ________ under the desk.

4 ________ on the table. ________ under the desk.

5 ________ on the desk. ________ on the bed.

5904 6 Barnabas ________ in his basket. He ________.

5 Saturday afternoon (was/were in questions and short answers)

▸ p. 86 • GF 18 (p. 141)

Where were they on Saturday afternoon? Write questions with **was** *or* **were** *and short answers:*
Yes, he was. / No, they weren't. / …

1 Jo/at the sports shop?
Was Jo at the sports shop? – Yes, he was.

2 Sophie and Emily/at the café?
Were Sophie and Emily at home? – No, they weren't. They were at the swimming pool.

3 Jack/at the pet shop?

4 Tim and Florian/at a football match?

5 Ananda/at the café?

6 Becky and Lucy/at home?

6005

• Now you

Where were you and your family (mum/dad/brother/sister) or your friends last Saturday afternoon? At the shops? At your grandma's house? … Write four sentences.

Last Saturday afternoon I was at

6 WORDS What are the words? ► p. 87

a) *Find and write the missing letters.*

ou | au | eo | ea | ei | oi | ai

reh ea rsal – sh ___ t – n ___ se – bec ___ se – w ___ t – r ___ dy

n ___ ghb ___ r – p ___ ple – s ___ nd – with ___ t – ch ___ r – upst ___ rs

b) *Now fill in correct forms from a).*

Jack: The ______________ was fantastic. Our band played two songs ______________ a mistake. Miss White says we ______________ great. My parents can't ______________ to see the show. Lots of ______________ want to come, our ______________ too. Jo sings in the ______________.

6106 He makes lots of ______________, and sings all the time.

○ 7 A verb snake (Simple past: regular verbs) ► p. 87 • GF 19a (p. 142)

Find and colour the verbs in the verb snake. Then write them in the simple past.

shouted, liked, ______________________________

____

8 PRONUNCIATION Word CDs (Past forms) ► p. 87 • GF 19a (p. 142) 7

a) *Listen to the words. Where can you hear the extra syllable –ed* [ɪd]*? Colour the CDs red or blue.*
Red = extra syllable: needed ['niːdɪd]. *Blue = no extra syllable: called* [kɔːld].

needed | called | painted 1 | worked 2 | added 3 | used 4

waited 5 | shouted 6 | watched 7 | started 8 | hated 9

b) *Now add the numbers of all the red CDs. Is your answer '32'? Correct!*

9 Last week (Simple past: regular verbs in positive statements)

► p. 87 • GF 19a (p. 142)

Look at Tim's notes for last week. Then write sentences.

Mon – clean dad's car ✓
Tue – walk to school – no bike ✓
Wed – help Alex with Maths ✓
Thur – call Florian and Ed ✓
Fri – watch DVDs with Florian ✓
Sat – play cards with Ed ✓

On Monday he cleaned his dad's car.
On Tuesday he ____________________.
On ____________________
____
____
____

10 Match the pieces (Simple past: irregular verbs in positive statements)

► p. 88 • GF 19b (p. 142)

○ ***a)*** *Find, colour and write the pairs.*

Infinitive:	Simple past:
have	had
go	

b) *Now complete the story about Tim with verbs from a).*

Last Saturday Tim __________ a big breakfast. Then he __________ to the park.

Becky __________, 'Mum isn't here. Lunch is at twelve. Don't be late!'

Tim's friends __________ to the park with their skateboards. They all __________ a really good time.

Suddenly Tim __________, 'Oh, no! It's one o'clock. I'm late!' At home Becky __________,'Sorry, Tim. You're too late for lunch, and I'm going now. But there's some food in the fridge.' Tim __________ to the fridge. Sandwiches? Chicken? Potato salad? But oh, no! Just cold chips!

● Now you

6210
6211

Write five or more sentences about your last weekend in your exercise book.
You can use ideas from exercises 9 and 10.
On Saturday I ... In the afternoon ... On Sunday we ...

11 REVISION He doesn't do that… (Simple present: negative statements) ▸ p. 88 • GF 7c (p. 134)

Complete the sentences about Barnabas.

Tim: Barnabas is a very good pet. He doesn't sleep (~~sleep~~) all day and he ______ (~~eat~~) too much. He ______ (~~take~~) fish from the fridge and he ______ (~~make~~) a mess.

Right! And I don't sit (~~sit~~) on the sofa.
I ______ (~~bring~~) sweet little mice into the house,
and I ______ (~~sleep~~) on Tim's bed. Right? Right!

12 They didn't do that … (Simple past: negative statements) ▸ p. 89 • GF 20 (p. 143)

Write what Tim's grandparents didn't do 60 years ago. Complete the sentences.

call • listen • play • watch • wear • write

1 They didn't wear jeans. They ______ computer games.

2 They ______ to rap music. They ______ people on mobile phones.

6312 *3* They ______ DVDs. They ______ e-mails.

Just for fun

Teacher: Jimmy, how do you spell 'Geography'?
Jimmy: G-e-o-g-r-a-f-y.
Teacher: The dictionary spells it with 'ph'.
Jimmy: You didn't ask me how the dictionary spells it.

Now you

Write what you/your family didn't do yesterday. Write four funny sentences.

My grandma didn't climb a tree yesterday. My dad didn't play hockey.

______

______

______

______

13 The Spring Show (Simple past: mixed forms) ▸ p. 89 • GF 19–20 (pp. 142–143)

Complete the sentences with simple past forms.

1 The Spring Show ___was___ (be) two days ago.

2 After the show Dan ________ (say), 'The pirate ship ________ (look) great.'

3 Sophie ________ (~~sing~~) in the show, but she ________ (dance).

4 Lots of parents ________ (come) to the show.

5 Poor Prunella. She ________ (~~see~~) the show.

6 The Spring Show ________ (~~be~~) just good. It ________ (be) fantastic!

○ 14 Questions and answers (Simple past) ▸ p. 89 • GF 21 (p. 143)

Match the questions and answers.
Then write the correct blue letter: t _ _ _ _ _ _. *What's the new word?*

1 Was the pirate scene good?	Yes, they were.	i
2 Were all the kids nervous?	No, they didn't.	k
3 Did Sophie dance in the show?	No, she wasn't.	e
4 Did Jack and Ananda sing?	No, he didn't.	t
5 Was Prunella at the show?	Yes, she did.	c
6 Did Jo play in the band?	Yes, it was.	▶ t

15 WORDS What's wrong? ▸ p. 89

Look at the boxes and write the correct words in the puzzle. Then find the word down.

1 gzeanmia | 3 yps | 7 xlpemae | 2 miorinoftan

4 rdeti | 6 nkgi | 5 tlarcie

Dilip buys a music (1) … every week. ☐☐☐☐☐☐☐☐

Here's some (2) … from the German school. ☐☐☐☐☐☐☐☐☐☐☐

Maybe Mr Green is a bank robber or a (3) … ☐☐☐

Dan is going to bed. He's really (4) … ☐☐☐☐☐

Ananda had an (5) … in the school magazine. ☐☐☐☐☐☐☐

Who was the pirate (6) … in the Spring Show? ☐☐☐☐

What's a verb? Give me an (7) … , please. ☐☐☐☐☐☐☐

6415 **Did you do this exercise without a** ☐☐☐☐☐☐☐ ?

16 STUDY SKILLS Unbekannte Wörter verstehen ▸ p. 96 • SF 6 (p. 124)

a) *Markiere die unbekannten Wörter gelb.*

Becky On my birthday Mum and Dad want to go with us to London to see a musical.
Tim Oh, no! That sounds boring!
Becky It's my birthday and I want to see The Phantom of the Opera. So be quiet and listen. This is what it says in my magazine.

The Phantom of the Opera by Andrew Lloyd Webber is a tragic love story. The scene is Paris, in the year 1911. The phantom – a mysterious musical genius with a wonderful voice – wears a mask because his face is ugly. He lives under the Opera House, under the streets of Paris where people can't see him. Christine, a beautiful young opera singer, is taking lessons from a mysterious new teacher – the Phantom. He loves Christine, but she doesn't love him.

Tim Romantic stuff! Girls! That isn't for me.
Becky Tim, be quiet and listen!

He wants to make her into the next big star of the Opera. Christine calls the phantom 'the angel of music', but she is afraid of him because he is a very strict teacher. Bad things happen at the Opera House. Suddenly somebody is dead. One day, Christine pulls the mask from the Phantom's face and ...

Tim Wow! Is he a real person or is he a ghost? Is he really ugly and scary without his mask? Cool! Let's go to see The Phantom of the Opera!

No, no! No phantoms! What about Clever Cats? Yes, Clever Cats.

b) *Wie kannst du diese Wörter erschließen? Manchmal treffen zwei Kästchen zu. Setze Häkchen (✓):*

	Bild	ähnliches deutsches Wort	Zusammenhang
phantom	☐	☑	☐
mask	☐	☐	☐
strict	☐	☐	☐
ugly	☐	☐	☐

c) *Schreib drei Wörter auf, die du durch die Bilder erschließen kannst.*

ugly (hässlich), ______________________

d) *Schreib fünf Wörter auf, die im Deutschen ähnlich sind. Schreib auch das deutsche Wort auf.*

phantom (Phantom), ______________________

____

____

e) *Welche Wörter kannst du aus dem Zusammenhang erschließen?*

strict (streng), ______________________

____

f) *Schau dir deine markierten Wörter noch einmal an. Kannst du jetzt alle Wörter verstehen?*

17 WORKING WITH THE TEXT A pirate story ▸ pp. 96–98

a) *Look at pages 96–98 of your student's book again. Match the pictures and the titles A–D.*

A The cabin boy is scared
B Bonny finds out about the Silver Swordfish
C A happy ending for the real Jonah
D The pirates' terrible work

1 ☐

2 ☐

3 ☐

4 ☐

b) *What's wrong? Mark the wrong sentences and correct them.*

1 It was a dark and windy night. The ships were in the harbour. Only two sailors from the Silver Swordfish were in the tavern.

Only two sailors ______________________________.

2 Bonny and Captain Rackham climbed onto the Silver Swordfish. They had pistols and swords. They wanted to help the sailors on the ship.

They wanted ______________________________.

3 The cabin boy cleaned the Captain's cabin. Then he was tired, so he was soon asleep. Suddenly Bonny saw him and said, 'Good luck for you, boy!'

Bonny said, ______________________________!'

4 Jonah was cold and scared. He opened his eyes. He was still on the floor of the cabin.

He was ______________________________.

c) *Now you are Jo. Tell Dan about your dream in the simple past. Use the notes or your own ideas.*

1 I/be/cabin boy/pirate ship • 2 First/Captain and Bonny/kill/two sailors/Silver Swordfish • 3 In cabin/I see/that/Bonny/be/woman • 4 After that/pirates/want to/kill me • 5 I/be/on the plank!

I was a cabin boy on a pirate ship.

____

____

____

6617
6618

1 Fill in: *was* (2x), *were*, *wasn't*, *weren't*

There ______________ a pet show in Bristol last week.

There ______________ some beautiful cats – but they ______________ very clever. One cat ______________ beautiful – but he ______________ very clever ... Look!

2 Yesterday

Complete the sentences with verbs in the simple past.

1 Sophie ______________ her bike.

2 Toby ______________ to his judo lesson.

3 Did Jo ______________ after ten o'clock?

4 Tim and Florian ______________ a chocolate cake.

5 Dilip ______________ the guitar.

6 Becky and Lucy ______________ their friends.

1

clean

2

~~go~~

3

get up

4

make

5

~~practise~~

6

call

3 Clubs and activities

Where can you do these things? Complete the sentences.

1 You can act in plays in the ______________.

2 You can paint pictures in the ______________.

3 You can sing songs in the ______________.

4 You can do jazz dance in the ______________.

5 You can play the clarinet in the ______________.

16 points

• Now you

Write an e-mail to a friend about what you did last weekend in your exercise book. Use the simple past. Ideas: do sport, see friends, have visitors, go to the park/the shops, watch TV/DVDs ...

Dear ...

6704
6705

I had a great weekend. On Friday I ...

Unit 6 Great places for kids

1 WORDS Places to go ▸ pp. 100–101

a) *Where did Florian and his cousin go? Fill in the missing words from the box.*

bridge • café (2x) • church • *city* • museum • park • station • tower • village

I live in Bristol. It's a big *city*. Yesterday I went to see my cousin Leo. He lives in a __________ – well, it's a little town really. Leo came to the __________ to meet me. It was a hot day, so we went to a __________ for a drink first. Then we went to the __________. We saw lots of interesting things for kids, like old cars and funny bikes. The museum was next to a nice old __________. It had a big __________ with a bell. After that we went to the __________ and watched some kids on their skateboards. We walked over the little __________ and watched the fish in the water. Then Leo wanted a cola, so we went to the __________ again for a cola and a very big ice cream.

b) *Would you like to go to these places with a friend? Why? Why not? Write about two pictures. Start with:* **I'd like to go to …** *or* **I wouldn't like to go to …**

I'd like to go to the tower. You can climb it and look at the streets from the top.

____

____

____

____

____

6800
6801

2 WORDS Word bridges ▸ p. 102

a) *How many words can you make from the word bridges? Use the Dictionary in your student's book (pp. 179–191).*

c ⌒ e cage, café, ______________________

____

h ⌒ e horse, ______________________

e ⌒ e eye, ______________________

b) *Now think of more bridges with different first and last letters. Write them in your exercise book.*

3 Extra What are they going to do? (going to-future) ▸ p. 103 • GF 22 (p. 144)

Match and write sentence pairs.

Sophie is thirsty. Jack's homework is boring. Jo and Dan are hungry. Tim and Florian like football. Barnabas is tired.	They He She	is/are going to	sleep on the sofa. have a drink. read a spy story. make some sandwiches. watch a match on TV.

Sophie is thirsty. She's going to have a drink.

____

____

____

6903 ______________________

4 REVISION No, you didn't, Prunella! (Simple past: negative statements) ▸ p. 103 • GF 20 (p. 143)

What does Sophie say? Write her sentences.

Prunella When I was a real girl 200 years ago,
I went to school on my bike.

Sophie Prunella, you didn't go to school on your bike.

Prunella:	***Sophie:***
1 I watched TV every evening.	Oh, no. You didn't ______________________.
2 I had an MP3 player.	That's silly[1]. You ______________________.
3 I played computer games.	No! ______________________.
4 I collected phone cards.	Prunella, ______________________.
5 I went to judo lessons.	And ______________________.

[1] silly ['sɪli] *albern, dumm*

5 Sophie likes the library because ... (Word order in subordinate clauses)

► p. 103 • GF 23 (p. 145)

a) *Match and write correct sentences with* **because** *or* **when**.

Sophie likes the library		people argue.
Dan hates it	because	*it's really quiet.*
Prunella doesn't get up late	when	she doesn't sleep.
Ananda doesn't like it		Jo sings the pirate song.

1 *Sophie likes the library because it's really quiet.*

2 ______________________________

3 ______________________________

4 ______________________________

Just for fun

What do you say when you meet a monster with two heads?[1]

b) *Now write sentences about Barnabas with the words in the correct order.*

1 Barnabas is always happy when ... (him/Tim/feeds).

Barnabas ______________________________

______________________________.

2 Tim hates it when ... (on his face/Barnabas/sits).

____

____

3 The neighbour throws water at Barnabas because ... (in his garden/cats/he/doesn't like).

____

____

7005 ______________________________

Now you

Complete the sentences.

My mum isn't happy when ______________________________.

I never go ______________ because ______________

______________________________.

My teacher doesn't like it when ______________________________

______________________________.

I don't eat ______________ because ______________.

[1] Hello, hello.

6 WORDS Good and bad words ▸ p. 103

a) *Which are good* ☺ *words? Write them in* ***green****. Which are bad* ☹ *words? Write them in* ***red****.*

be afraid • bad • beautiful • boring • danger • dead • difficult • easy • fun • great • happy • interesting • poor • pretty • smile • scary • terrible

be afraid, bad, beautiful,

b) *Add more* ***good*** *and* ***bad*** *words in your exercise book.*

7 These aren't my things (this, that, these, those) ▸ p. 103

The twins' things are all in the wrong places. What does Jo say about his things? Use ***this****,* ***that****,* ***these****,* ***those****.*

1 *This isn't my sweatshirt. That's my sweatshirt* on Dan's bed.

2 ______ on Dan's chair.

3 *These aren't* ______ over there in the corner.

4 ______ on the floor.

5 ______ on Dan's bed.

7107 6 ______ on Dan's shelf.

8 PRONUNCIATION [ʃ], [tʃ] and [dʒ] ▸ p. 103 8

Listen to the CD and colour the [ʃ]-words ***red****, the [tʃ]-words* ***blue*** *and the [dʒ]-words* ***green****.*

Look: [ʃ] ship [tʃ] chips [dʒ] job

1 information – juice	4 church – Geography
2 check – finish	5 bridge – shout
3 village – chicken	6 chair – chocolate

9 REVISION A scary story? (Simple present, adverbs)

▸ p. 104 • GF 7 (pp. 132–134), 10–11 (pp. 136–137)

a) *Complete the sentences. Use the simple present.*

Florian Do you know any scary stories? I like them a lot.

Tim Well, maybe we ________ (have got) a poltergeist in our house. Becky ________ (often/hear) loud noises in the night and my mum ________ (say) somebody ________ (sometimes/make) a mess in the kitchen. She ________ (often/see) cake or cheese on the floor the next morning.

Florian Wow! A real poltergeist? Fantastic! What ________ (he/do)? Where ________ (he/go)? ________ (he/drop) plates?

Tim Well, he ________ (do) really bad things. He ________ (always/go) to the kitchen and ________ (eat). But poltergeists ________ (eat). Hmmm. You know what? I ________ (think) our poltergeist ________ (be) my dad!

b) *Draw a picture of a funny ghost[1] in your exercise book. Write six sentences about what he* **does** *and* **doesn't do**.
He makes loud noises in the night. He doesn't sleep ...

10 REVISION A school trip (Present progressive)

▸ p. 104 • GF 15–16a (p. 140)

Lucy is on a school trip. She writes to her family. Use these verbs in the present progressive: **have, sit, wear, swim, play, take, talk**

Hi, Mum and Dad

It's great here. Here's a photo of me with my classmates.
Mark is swimming in the pool.
Dave and Emma ________ cards.
Rob ________ next to me – with the big ice cream. Kim and Ann ________ to the teachers. Mr Fox ________ sunglasses. He looks like Will Smith! You can't see Nina because she ________ the photo.
We ________ lots of fun.

See you soon
Lucy

7210

Rhyme time

At the end of our road
There's a funny old house,
Its door is black and red.
In the funny old house
lives a funny old ghost[1],
Oh no! He's under my bed!

[1] ghost [gəʊst] *Gespenst, Geist*

11 What's different? (Simple present and present progressive)

▸ p. 104 • GF 24 (pp. 145–146)

Today is different. What do the students and teachers usually do? What are they doing today? Circle the correct verb form.

On Fridays at 10.50 Form 7PK usually (has / is having) Maths, but today the students (are playing / play) a game. Form 7BW usually (does / is doing) exercises in the French lesson, but today the students (sing / are singing) songs. They always (listen / are listening) to their teachers, but now they (don't listen / aren't listening) – they (make / are making) a terrible noise. The students never (eat / are eating) in class but now they (are eating / eat) ice cream. They (are having / have) lots of fun. And Mr Kingsley (doesn't shout / isn't shouting) today. He's happy. Why? Well, it's the last day of school before the holidays!

12 Who's who? (Simple present and present progressive)

▸ p. 104 • GF 24 (pp. 145–146)

a) *Read about the five friends. Write the verbs in the simple present or present progressive.*

Maria likes (like) hamburgers, but today she is eating (eat) sandwiches.

Sally ________ (~~read~~) many books. She ________ (usually/buy) magazines or comics.

Liz ________ (wear) her new sunglasses today. She ________ (eat) a big ice cream.

Jane ________ (like) books. She ________ (read) a great detective story now.

Sarah ________ (~~like~~) sweet things.

○ ***b)*** *Who's who? Write their names.*

Number 1 is Maria. Number 3 is ________. Number 5 is ________.

312 Number 2 is ________. Number 4 is ________.

13 REVISION *There*, *their* or *they're* ▸ p. 105

Jo Where are my football boots?

Dan ___________ over _______________ .

Jo No, they aren't. Mike and Leo

put ___________ boots over ___________ .

Dan Mmm. Right. They can't be your

boots. _____________ clean.

14 WORDS A puzzle ▸ p. 105

a) *Complete the sentences.*

1 It's fun to e x p l o r e new places.

2 Do you live in a town, a city or a v _ _ _ _ _ _ _ ?

3 *Mr Kingsley:* Well, we've got time for _ _ _ _ o _ _ presentation.

4 The library is usually quiet. We have to w _ _ _ _ _ _ _ !

5 *Sophie:* I hate it when people don't _ _ _ _ _ h their sentences.

b) *Write a new word with the letters in the blue boxes from a). The word is:* _ _ _ _ e .

15 REVISION Getting by in English ▸ p. 105

Your neighbours have got visitors, a boy and a girl from England. You meet the English girl, Jenny, on the street. She doesn't understand German. Ask her questions in English.

Frag sie ...

..., woher sie kommt. *Where are you from?*

..., wie alt sie ist. ______________________

..., ob sie Sport mag. ______________________

..., ob ihr Bruder Sport mag. ______________________

..., ob sie ein Haustier hat. ______________________

..., ob sie Gitarre spielt. ______________________

..., wer ihre Lieblingsband ist. ______________________

..., ob sie deine CDs hören möchte. ______________________

..., ob sie mit dir am Freitag auf eine Party gehen möchte. ______________________

7415

16 Just for fun ▸ p. 111

Read the jokes.

(1) Here are my favourite jokes:
A Hi! Are you coming to my party?
B No, I'm not. I'm going to see *Harry Potter.*
A Well, you can bring him too!

(2)
A: What date is it?
B: I don't know. Look at that newspaper on the chair.
A: But that's yesterday's newspaper ...

(3) I know some good jokes too:
What do elephants do in their free time?
– They watch elevision!

(4)
Teacher Say a sentence with 'I'.
Jimmy I is ...
Teacher No, no, Jimmy. That's wrong. You must say 'I am ...'
Jimmy OK. I am the ninth letter of the alphabet.

(5) Now it's my turn:
A I've got an invitation to Mike's party, but I can't go.
B Why not?
A Well, it says from 5 to 9 – and I'm 11.

(6) And here's another:
How do you know that carrots are good for your eyes?
– Because rabbits don't wear glasses.

(7) Here's my first joke:
What has got forty feet and sings?
– A school choir.

(8) My next joke is better:
A: Our dog is very brave[1]. He brings the newspaper for us every morning.
B: Why is that brave?
A: Because it's the neighbours' newspaper.

9 And now here's the best joke!
What do cats eat on a hot day?
– Mice cream! Ha-ha-ha!

Now you

Which jokes are funny or silly[2]? Which is your favourite? Which jokes don't you like? Write in your exercise book.

My favourite joke is number ... because ... ***I don't like Lucy's first joke because ...***

[1] brave [breɪv] *tapfer, mutig* [2] silly ['sɪli] *dumm, albern*

1 Places: write the names.

1 ______________ 3 ______________

2 ______________ 4 ______________

2 What's right? Write correct sentences.

1 Presentations are fun ... (because/can/you/in groups/work).

____

2 The kids saw some great things ... (when/to the museum/they/went).

____

3 Sophie argued ... (because/used/too much glue/Ananda/for the poster).

____

4 Ananda hates it ... (when/argue/people/all the time).

____

3 Fill in ***this***, ***that***, ***these*** and ***those***.

Dan: No, it's wrong. ______________ is your cola

and ______________ are your chips.

______________ orange juice is for me, and

______________ are my sandwiches.

4 Circle the correct verb form.

Lucy I (usually go / 'm usually going) to my guitar lesson on Tuesdays. But this week

I (go / 'm going) on Wednesday. What about you?

Tim Well, we (don't have / aren't having) Maths homework on Wednesdays,

but I (do / 'm doing) my Maths homework today because it was for yesterday...

16 points

• Now you

7605
7606

Write about your city, town or village. What is there in your town? Ideas: houses, flats, cafés, shops, churches, museums, libraries, schools, parks, sports clubs. Write in your exercise book.

You can use these words: ***I live in ... It's a nice ... My favourite place is ... There are lots of ... We've got ...***

Jetzt kann ich ...

	Sehr gut!	OK	Verbessern!
HÖREN: Ich kann ...			
... Arbeitsanweisungen und Fragen im Unterricht verstehen.	☐	☐	☐
... Fragen über meine Freizeit, Schulklubs und meine Stadt verstehen.	☐	☐	☐
... die Auflösung der SHoCK-Team-Geschichte in Unit 6 verstehen.	☐	☐	☐
SPRECHEN: Ich kann ...			
... verschiedene Lebensmittel und Getränke nennen.	☐	☐	☐
... mit *I'd like* sagen, was ich haben möchte.	☐	☐	☐
... mit dem *present progressive* sagen, was jemand gerade tut oder was gerade geschieht.	☐	☐	☐
... mit dem *simple past* sagen, was in der Vergangenheit war oder geschah.	☐	☐	☐
... die Wörter der Units 4–6 richtig aussprechen.	☐	☐	☐
... die Geschichte vom SHoCK-Team in groben Zügen nacherzählen.	☐	☐	☐
LESEN: Ich kann ...			
... die Arbeitsanweisungen in meinem Buch/Workbook verstehen.	☐	☐	☐
... die Texte der Units 4–6 lesen und verstehen.	☐	☐	☐
SCHREIBEN: Ich kann ...			
... eine Einkaufsliste für Lebensmittel und Getränke schreiben.	☐	☐	☐
... einen kleinen Text über meine Stadt schreiben.	☐	☐	☐
... eine kurze E-Mail schreiben.	☐	☐	☐
... eine Einladung zu einer Party oder einem Grillfest schreiben.	☐	☐	☐
... *some* und *any* richtig benutzen.	☐	☐	☐
LAND UND LEUTE: Ich weiß ...			
..., was es für Klubs und Aktivitäten in britischen Schulen gibt.	☐	☐	☐
..., wie sich der britische Schulalltag vom deutschen unterscheidet.	☐	☐	☐
LERNEN UND ARBEITEN: Ich kann ...			
... mit meiner Lieblingsmethode Vokabeln selbstständig lernen.	☐	☐	☐
... einfache Notizen nach *key words* anfertigen.	☐	☐	☐
... auf verschiedene Weise unbekannte Wörter erschließen.	☐	☐	☐
... mit drei anderen zusammen eine *placemat activity* bearbeiten.	☐	☐	☐

WIE ICH MICH VERBESSERN KÖNNTE: Ich könnte ...

- ... häufiger im Dictionary nachschlagen. ☐
- ... häufiger im Skills File lesen. ☐
- ... häufiger im Grammar File nachschauen. ☐
- ... nützliche Sätze für bestimmte Situationen auswendig lernen. ☐
- ... kurze Texte aus meinem Buch abschreiben. ☐
- ... mit einem Partner oder zu dritt Rollenspiele einüben. ☐
- ... eine/n englische/n E-Freund/in suchen. ☐

- Hier kannst du deine Antworten im Checkpoint überprüfen. Falls du Probleme mit den jeweiligen Aufgaben hattest, folge den Lernhilfen in der rechten Spalte. Die Verweise beziehen sich auf dein Schülerbuch oder dein Workbook.
- Deine Punktzahl kannst du ermitteln, indem du dir für jede richtige Lösung einen Punkt gibst. Schreib deine Gesamtpunktzahl in das gelbe Kästchen unten links.

1 What can you see in the classroom?

1 window
2 board
3 timetable
4 calendar
5 teacher
6 table
7 apple
8 chair

8 P.

- Schau dir Skills File 1 zu „Wörter lernen" (S. 118–119) noch einmal an.
- Lern die Wörter mithilfe des Vocabulary (S. 154–158).

2 Complete.

1 Barnabas isn't a parrot.
He 's a cat.
2 'I 'm a very nice pet.
I 'm not a mad cat!'
3 They aren't classmates.
They 're brother and sister.

6 P.

- Die Formen von *be* kannst du dir im Grammar File 2a (S. 128) noch einmal ansehen.
- Löse die Aufgaben 3 und 4 im Practice-Teil (S. 26), um die Formen von *be* sicher zu verwenden.

3 Write what they *have got* and what they *haven't got*.

1 The Hansons have got a B&B. It has got five rooms.
2 The Kapoors haven't got a house. They have got a flat and a shop.
3 Ananda has got a brother, but she hasn't got a pet.

6 P.

- Lern die Formen von *have got* mithilfe des Grammar File 5a (S. 130).
- Wiederhole die Übung 12a–b zu *have got* im Practice-Teil (S. 30).

Now you (Musterlösung)

Hi!
I'm your new friend from Germany. My name is Heike and I'm from Kassel. I'm 11 years old. I've got a brother, Markus. He's 13. My favourite sport is basketball. I can play badminton too. My favourite subjects are Maths and Music. I've got a dog, Benno. Have you got a pet?
Bye!

- Falls du Schwierigkeiten hattest, einen zusammenhängenden Text zu schreiben, schau dir in deinem Workbook die Aufgabe 22 (S. 20) noch einmal an und schreib den Text von Jo in dein Heft.
- Lern die Formen von *be* (Grammar File 2a, S. 128), *can* (Grammar File 3a, S. 129) und *have got* (Grammar File 5a, S. 130).

Ich habe ______ Punkte von 20.

20–17: Sehr gut. Weiter so!
16–13: Schon recht gut.
Unter 13: Genauer lernen!

1 What are they? Label the pets.

1 *budgie*
2 *rabbit*
3 *mouse*
4 *tortoise*
5 *guinea pig*
6 *horse*

6 P.

2 *'s* or *s'*?

1 The (Kapoors) *Kapoors'* flat is over the shop.
2 7PK is (Mr Kingsley) *Mr Kingsley's* form.
3 Bill and Ben are (Dan and Jo) *Dan and Jo's* pets.
4 Barnabas is (Tim) *Tim's* cat.

4 P.

3 *His*, *her*, *its* or *their*?

1 The Carter-Browns and all *their* pets are at home today.
2 Prunella is at home. Sophie's room is *her* room too.
3 Jack is in the park with *his* dad.
4 Sophie's cousin Emma has got a tortoise. What's *its* name?

4 P.

4 Complete the sentences with: *like*, *likes* (✓), *doesn't like*, *don't like* (✗)

1 Lucy *likes* horses and fish. She *doesn't like* cats.
2 Jo and Tim *don't like* fish, but they *like* horses and cats.
3 Florian *doesn't like* fish or cats.
4 Becky *likes* all the pets.

6 P.

Now you (Musterlösung)

I've got a hamster. His name is Nick. He's brown and white. He eats hamster food and carrots. He lives in a nice cage in the living room. My friend has got a cat. Her name is Pam. She's black and white. She eats cat food and fish. I like dogs, cats, horses and hamsters. I don't like fish or budgies.

Ich habe ____ Punkte von 20.

20–17: Sehr gut. Weiter so!
16–13: Schon recht gut.
Unter 13: Genauer lernen!

Falls du Probleme hattest:

- Schau dir Skills File 1 zu „Wörter lernen“ (S. 118–119) noch einmal an.
- Lern die Vokabeln noch einmal (S. 159).

- Wie du *'s* und *s'* richtig benutzt, kannst du im Grammar File 9 (S. 135) nachlesen.
- Löse die Aufgabe 15 im Practice-Teil (S. 47) noch einmal, um den *s*-Genitiv zu üben.

- Die Possessivbegleiter findest du im Grammar File 8 (S. 134–135).
- Wiederhole die Übung 14a–b im Practice-Teil (S. 46), um die Possessivbegleiter sicher zu benutzen.

- Schau dir Grammar File 7a und 7c (S. 132–134) an, um die positiven und negativen Formen im *simple present* zu lernen.
- Löse die Aufgaben 4 (S. 42), 6a (S. 43) und 10–11a (S. 45) im Practice-Teil.

- Falls du Schwierigkeiten hattest, einen zusammenhängenden Text zu schreiben, lies dir Skills File 3 zu Mindmaps (S. 121) durch. Dort erfährst du, wie du deine Ideen für einen Text sammeln und ordnen kannst.
- Die Formen von *have got* findest du im Grammar File 5a (S. 130).
- *Simple present*-Formen kannst du im Grammar File 7a und 7c (S. 132–134) nachschlagen.

1 Sports and hobbies

1 Jack *makes models* .

2 Sophie *goes riding* .

3 Dilip *plays the guitar* .

4 P. 4 Ananda *collects stamps* .

2 Ask about the people in ( ).

1 *Do Dan and Sophie like music?*

2 *Does Sophie play tennis?*

3 *Do you write e-mails?*

4 P. 4 *Does Jack's dad do yoga?*

3 Make correct sentences.

1 *Jay never goes to football matches.*

2 *I don't often write e-mails.*

3 *Does Becky play basketball?*

4 P. 4 *Where does Prunella play tennis?*

4 Write what they *have to* do or *don't have to* do.

1 At school we *have to* listen to the teacher.

2 Most days Jack *has to* help at the B&B.

3 In the holidays we *don't have to* get up early.

4 P. 4 Prunella *doesn't have to* go to school.

Now you (Musterlösung)

I like sport. I play football at school and I do judo on Tuesdays. I collect posters for my room too. My friend plays basketball and he makes models. My dad plays tennis and my mum plays the piano. My sister goes riding and she collects DVDs.

Ich habe [ ] Punkte von 16.

16–14: Sehr gut. Weiter so!
13–11: Schon recht gut.
Unter 11: Genauer lernen!

Falls du Probleme hattest:

- Schau dir Skills File 1 zu „Wörter lernen“ (S. 118–119) noch einmal an.
- Lern die Wörter mithilfe des Vocabulary (S. 164–165).
- Löse die Aufgaben 1a und 2a–b und schau dir deine Mindmap zu Aufgabe 3 noch einmal an (Practice-Teil S. 58).

- Wie du Fragen im *simple present* richtig bildest, erfährst du im Grammar File 10a (S. 136).
- Wiederhole die Übungen 5 und 6a im Practice-Teil (S. 59).

- Lies Grammar File 10–11 (S. 136–137).
- Löse die Aufgaben 5, 6a (S. 59) und 14a (S. 63) im Practice-Teil.

- Schau dir Grammar File 12 zu *have to* (S. 138) an.
- Übe die Formen von *have to* mithilfe der Aufgabe 16 im Practice-Teil (S. 63).

- Falls du Schwierigkeiten hattest, einen Text zu schreiben, lies dir Skills File 3 zu Mindmaps (S. 121) noch einmal durch.
- Grammar File 7 (S. 132–134) verdeutlicht dir noch einmal den Gebrauch des *simple present*.

1 What does Mrs Carter-Brown need from the shops?

1 *cheese* 4 *orange juice*

2 *lemonade* 5 *sausages*

6 P. 3 *chicken* 6 *ice cream*

2 Complete with: *me*, *him*, *her*, *it*, *them*

1 *Tim* Where's Mum's shopping list? I can't find *it*.

2 *Becky* I don't know. Don't ask *me*.

3 *Tim* Well, where's Mum? Let's ask *her*.

4 *Becky* Where are Mum and Dad? I can't see *them*.

5 P. 5 *Tim* Dad is in the garden. Let's ask *him*.

3 What's in the fridge? *Some* or *any*?

1 *Tim* There's *some* fruit, but there aren't *any* carrots.

2 *Becky* And is there *any* milk?

4 P. 3 *Tim* No, but there's *some* lemonade.

4 What*'s happening* at the station?

1 A man *is reading* a newspaper.

2 Two girls *are getting on* the train.

3 A boy *is calling* somebody on his mobile.

4 A woman *is giving* a girl some money.

5 P. 5 Two boys *are running* to the train.

● **Now you** (Musterlösung)

I'm having a big barbecue for my birthday. All my friends and classmates are here. They're giving me presents. There's great food. We're eating chicken, sausages and potato salad. My friends are singing 'Happy birthday to you'. Now we're dancing. The music is fantastic. We're having a great time.

Ich habe ☐ Punkte von 20.

20–17: Sehr gut. Weiter so!
16–13: Schon recht gut.
Unter 13: Genauer lernen!

Falls du Probleme hattest:

- Schau dir Skills File 1 zu „Wörter lernen" (S. 118–119) noch einmal an.
- Lern die Vokabeln (S. 169–170).

- Die Objektformen der Personalpronomen findest du im Grammar File 13 (S. 138–139).
- Üben kannst du sie mithilfe der Aufgaben 3 und 4 im Practice-Teil (S. 75–76).

- Wie du *some* und *any* richtig verwendest, zeigt dir Grammar File 14 (S. 139).
- Löse die Aufgabe 7 im Practice-Teil (S. 77).

- In den Grammar Files 15–16 (S. 140–141) kannst du nachlesen, wann du das *present progressive* benutzt und wie du die Formen bildest.
- Wiederhole die Aufgaben 9–11 im Practice-Teil (S. 78).

- Falls du Schwierigkeiten hattest, einen Text zu schreiben, schau dir die Aufgaben 13 (S. 54) und 18 (S. 56) in deinem Workbook noch einmal an und schreib den Text von 18a ab.
- Im Grammar File 7 (S. 132–134) findest du Informationen zum *simple present* und die Grammar Files 15–16 (S. 140–141) zeigen dir den Gebrauch des *present progressive.*

1 Fill in: *was* (2x), *were*, *wasn't*, *weren't*

There ___was___ a pet show in Bristol last week.

There ___were___ some beautiful cats – but they ___weren't___ very clever.

One cat ___wasn't___ beautiful – but he

5 P. ___was___ very clever ... Look!

2 Yesterday

1 Sophie ___cleaned___ her bike.

2 Toby ___didn't go___ to his judo lesson.

3 Did Jo ___get up___ after ten o'clock?

4 Tim and Florian ___made___ a chocolate cake.

5 Dilip ___didn't practise___ the guitar.

6 P. *6* Becky and Lucy ___called___ their friends.

3 Clubs and activities

1 You can act in plays in the ___Drama Club___.

2 You can paint pictures in the ___Art Club___.

3 You can sing songs in the ___Junior Choir___.

4 You can do jazz dance in the ___Dance Club___.

5 P. *5* You can play the clarinet in the ___Junior Band___.

Now you (Musterlösung)

Dear ...
I had a great weekend. On Friday I went swimming with my friends. On Saturday we went to the shops and we had sausages and chips for lunch.
In the evening I watched a funny film on TV.
On Sunday I got up very late. My aunt and uncle came for lunch. After lunch we went to the park with our dog. Great!
School tomorrow – not so great.
Love ...

Ich habe ______ Punkte von 16.

16–14: Sehr gut. Weiter so!
13–11: Schon recht gut.
Unter 11: Genauer lernen!

Falls du Probleme hattest:

- Die *simple past*-Formen von *be* findest du im Grammar File 18 (S. 141).
- Die Aufgabe 2 im Practice-Teil (S. 90) bietet dir eine Übungsmöglichkeit dieser Formen.

- Schlag Grammar File 19 (S. 142) auf, um zu sehen, wie die regelmäßigen Formen im *simple past* gebildet werden und wie die unregelmäßigen Formen aussehen.
- Eine Liste von unregelmäßigen Verben findest du auf der S. 201 unten. Dort kannst du nachschauen, wenn dir eine Form nicht einfällt.
- Löse die Aufgaben 6 (S. 91), 9 (S. 92), 12a (S. 93) und 13–15 (S. 94) im Practice-Teil, um den Gebrauch des *simple past* besser zu beherrschen.

- Falls du vergessen hast, wie man die Namen der Klubs schreibt, dann schau dir in deinem Schülerbuch die S. 84–85 an.
- Such dort die Namen der Klubs und schreib sie in dein Heft.

- Falls du Schwierigkeiten hattest, deine Gedanken zu ordnen, schau dir Skills File 3 zu Mindmaps (S. 121) noch einmal an.
- Im Grammar File 19a (S. 142) findest du die Bildung von regelmäßigen Formen im *simple past*.
- Die unregelmäßigen Verben befinden sich im Grammar File 19b (S. 142) und auf der S. 201 unten.

1 Places: write the names.

1 *church* 3 *library*

4 P. 2 *bridge* 4 *tower*

2 What's right? Write correct sentences.

1 Presentations are fun ...
... because you can work in groups.

2 The kids saw some great things ...
... when they went to the museum.

3 Sophie argued ...
... because Ananda used too much glue for the poster.

4 Ananda hates it ...
4 P. *... when people argue all the time.*

3 Fill in *this*, *that*, *these* and *those*.

Dan: No, it's wrong. *This* is your cola and *these* are your chips. *That* orange juice is for me, and *those* are my sandwiches. 4 P.

4 Circle the correct verb form.

Lucy I (usually go / 'm usually going) to my guitar lesson on Tuesdays. But this week I (go / 'm going) on Wednesday. What about you?

Tim Well, we (don't have / aren't having) Maths homework on Wednesdays, but I (do / 'm doing) my Maths homework today because it was for yesterday... 4 P.

(Circled: usually go; 'm going; don't have; 'm doing)

Now you (Musterlösung)

I live in ... It's a nice town. There are great places for kids. In the town centre there are lots of shops. We've got a nice library too. It has got lots of books and DVDs. There's a nice café. My school is near the park. I often go to the park after school with my friends because we can play football there.

Ich habe ☐ Punkte von 16.

16–14: Sehr gut. Weiter so!
13–11: Schon recht gut.
Unter 11: Genauer lernen!

Falls du Probleme hattest:

- Lies Skills File 1 (S. 118–119).
- Lern die Wörter (S. 176–177).

- Schau dir die Wortstellung in Nebensätzen im Grammar File 23 (S. 145) an.
- Wiederhole die Übung 6 im Practice-Teil (S. 107).

- Lies den blauen Kasten im Vocabulary auf der S. 177 zu *this, that – these, those.*
- Löse die Aufgabe 7 im Practice-Teil (S. 108).

- Falls du nicht weißt, wann du die einfache Form der Gegenwart (*simple present*) und wann du die Verlaufsform (*present progressive*) verwenden musst, schau dir Grammar File 24 (S. 145–146) an.
- Übe den Gebrauch dieser beiden Formen mithilfe der Aufgaben 9, 11 und 12 im Practice-Teil (S. 108–109).

- Falls du zu wenig über deine Stadt oder dein Dorf weißt, kannst du versuchen, im Internet Informationen zu sammeln.
- Eine Mindmap (Skills File 3, S. 121) kann dir beim Sammeln und Ordnen deiner Gedanken behilflich sein.
- Den Gebrauch des *simple present* kannst du im Grammar File 7 (S. 132–134) und Grammar File 24 (S. 145–146) nachschlagen.

Unit 1

GF 1 Personal pronouns ▸ GF (p. 127)

Jack is nice. ▸ He's nice.
My pencil is red. ▸ It's red.

You are nice. = Du bist nett. / Ihr seid nett. / Sie sind nett.

Personalpronomen sind:
I, you, he, she, it, we, you, they.

Die deutschen Personalpronomen **du**, **ihr** und **Sie** heißen im Englischen alle ***you***.

Bei einer männlichen Person	– he	Bei einem Haustier	– he oder she
Bei einer weiblichen Person	– she	Bei einem Tier ohne Namen	– it
Bei einem Ding oder Begriff	– it	Bei mehreren Personen, Dingen, Tieren	– they

GF 2 The verb *(to) be* ▸ GF (p. 128)

a) Statements

Langformen: +	–	**Kurzformen:** +	–
I am	I am not	I'm	I'm not
you are	you are not	you're	you aren't
he/she/it is	he/she/it is not	he's/she's/it's	he/she/it isn't
we are	we are not	we're	we aren't
you are	you are not	you're	you aren't
they are	they are not	they're	they aren't

Beim Sprechen und in persönlichen Briefen werden meist die Kurzformen von *be* verwendet.

b) Questions

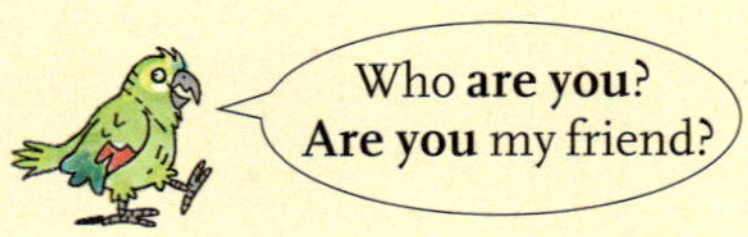

Fragen kannst du **mit Fragewort** *(Who …?)* oder **ohne Fragewort** *(Are you …?)* stellen.

Am I …? / Are you …? / Is he/she/it …?
Are we …? / Are you …? / Are they …?

Nach einem Fragewort wird *is* oft verkürzt:
Who's that? / Where's my book? / What's your name?

c) Short answers

+	–
Yes, I am.	No, I'm not.
Yes, you are.	No, you aren't.
Yes, he/she/it is.	No, he/she/it isn't.
Yes, we/you/they are.	No, we/you/they aren't.

! Nach *Yes* darfst du keine Kurzform verwenden.
Also nur
Yes, I am. / ***Yes, we are.***
usw.

GF 3 *can* ▸ GF (p. 129)

a) Statements

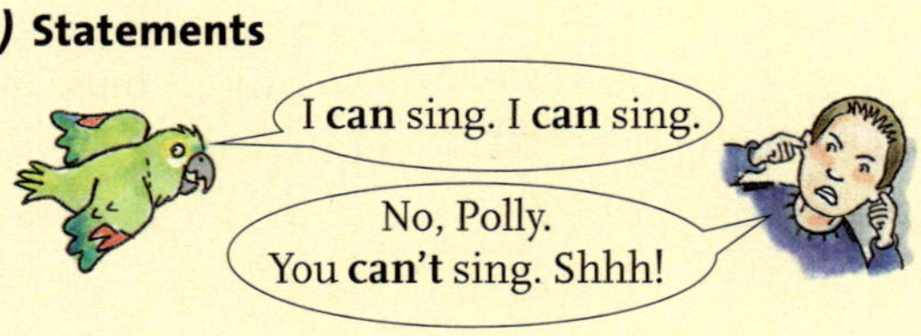

Mit *can* und *can't* drückst du aus, was jemand tun kann oder nicht tun kann.
Es gibt nur die Formen *can* bzw. *can't* für *I/you/he/she/it/we/they*.

b) Questions and short answers

Can you do tricks? – **Yes, I** can. / **No, I** can't.

◂ So bildest du Fragen und Kurzantworten mit *can* und *can't*.

GF 4 Imperatives ▸ GF (p. 130)

Write the words on the board, please.

Polly, don't sing. And don't talk, please.

Im Englischen gibt es nur eine Befehlsform, egal, mit wem du sprichst. Bei einem verneinten Befehl steht *don't* davor:
Don't walk. (Langform: *Do not walk.*)

GF 5 The verb *have got* ▸ *GF (pp. 130–131)*

a) Statements

Jack **has got** a parrot.

Sophie **hasn't got** a parrot. She**'s got** a dog.

Jo and Dan **have got** pets too.

Die Form *have got* gilt für *I, you, we* und *they*.
Bei *he/she/it* heißt die Form *has got*.

! – *She's got a dog.* = *She has got a dog.*
(nicht: *She ~~is~~ got a dog.*)
– *She's very nice.* = *She is very nice.*

Langformen: +	–	Kurzformen: +	–
I have got	I have not got	I've got	I haven't got
you have got	you have not got	you've got	you haven't got
he/she/it **has** got	he/she/it **has** not got	he**'s**/she**'s**/it**'s** got	he/she/it **hasn't** got
we have got	we have not got	we've got	we haven't got
you have got	you have not got	you've got	you haven't got
they have got	they have not got	they've got	they haven't got

b) Questions

Have you **got** a pet? / **Has** Jack **got** a pet?

! In Fragen steht *got* nach dem Subjekt (*you, Jack*).

Have I/you got ...?	**Has** he/she/it got ...?	Have we/you got ...?	Have they got ...?

c) Short answers

Have you got a pet? – **Yes, I have. / No, I haven't.**
Has Jack got a pet? – **Yes, he has.**

! **1** Bei der Kurzantwort fällt das *got* weg.
2 Nach *Yes* musst du immer die Langform verwenden.

Unit 2

GF 6 The plural of nouns ▸ *GF (pp. 131–132)*

a parrot
(Singular)

two parrot**s** [s]
(Plural)

Du bildest den Plural (die Mehrzahl) eines Nomens, indem du ein ***s*** an das Nomen anhängst: ***Singular + s = Plural***.

GF 7 The simple present ▸ *GF (pp. 132–134)*

a) Positive statements

I **get up**
at 7.15 every morning.
Then I **clean** my teeth.

◂ Jo redet hier über das, was er regelmäßig tut (*every morning*, „jeden Morgen"). Die Sätze stehen im *simple present*.

I/You	like	apples and bananas.
He/She/It	**likes**	
We/You/They	like	

Simple present?
He, she, it?
YES, YES! An **'s'**!

He, she, it –
das „**s**" muss mit!

c) Negative statements

I	don't	like	apples and bananas.
You	don't	like	
He/She/It	**doesn't**	**like**	
We/You/They	don't	like	

Polly says,
Please don't guess.
In *doesn't* + verb
there's just one **'s'**!

GF 8 Possessive determiners ▸ *GF (pp. 134–135)*

my	room	*mein Zimmer*	our	room	*unser Zimmer*
your	room	*dein/Ihr Zimmer*	your	room	*euer/Ihr Zimmer*
his	room	*sein Zimmer*	their	room	*ihr Zimmer*
her	room	*ihr Zimmer*			
its	room	*sein/ihr Zimmer*			

GF 9 The possessive form ▸ *GF (p. 135)*

Singular: Nomen + 's (the **dog's** basket)
Plural: Pluralform des Nomens + ' (the **rabbits'** hutch)

Wenn du sagen willst, dass etwas jemandem gehört (oder zu jemandem gehört), benutzt du den ***s*-Genitiv**.

! Anders als im Deutschen wird im Englischen das ***s*** mit einem Apostroph (**'**) angehängt.

Unit 3

GF 10 The simple present ▸ *GF (pp. 136–137)*

a) Yes/No questions

Do	I	like ...?	Do	we	like ...?
Do	you	like ...?	Do	you	like ...?
Does	he/she/it	like ...?	Do	they	like ...?

Polly says,
Please don't guess.
In questions with *Does*
there's just one 's'!

b) Short answers

Do you **get up** early? – **Yes, I** do. / **No, I** don't.
Does Jack **hate** sport? – **Yes, he** does.

Entscheidungsfragen werden nicht nur mit *Yes* oder *No* beantwortet, sondern mit einer Kurzantwort.

c) Questions with question words

When do you **play** tennis, Prunella?
And **where do** you **play**?

	Do	*you*	***play***	*tennis?*	(Entscheidungsfrage)
When	***do***	*you*	***play***	*tennis?*	(Fragen mit Fragewort: *When, Where, What, How, Why*)
How	***does***	*he*	***play***	*tennis?*	

GF 11 Adverbs of frequency: word order ▸ *GF (p. 137)*

I never **sleep**.
I usually **go** in all the rooms at night.

Jack always **writes** great stories.
Jack schreibt immer tolle Geschichten.

Prunella **can** often **help** Sophie.
Prunella kann Sophie oft helfen.

I**'m** usually nice to Sophie.

◂ Häufigkeitsadverbien (*always, usually, often, sometimes, never*) stehen gewöhnlich direkt **vor dem Vollverb** (z.B. *sleep, go*).

! Anders als im Deutschen stehen Häufigkeitsadverbien nie zwischen Verb und Objekt:

		Verb	Objekt			Verb		Objekt
Jo	*often*	***plays***	***football*** .		*Jo*	***spielt***	*oft*	***Fußball*** .

◂ Häufigkeitsadverbien stehen **hinter** *am/are/is*.

GF 12 The verb *(to) have to* ▸ *GF (p. 138)*

I **have to** get up early every day.
I **have to** help in the kitchen.

Wenn du ausdrücken willst, was du oder andere tun müssen, verwendest du *have to*.

+		–		?	
I/you	have to	I/you	don't have to	Do I/you	have to ...?
he/she/it	has to	he/she/it	doesn't have to	Does he/she/it	have to ...?
we/you/they	have to	we/you/they	don't have to	Do we/you/they	have to ...?

Unit 4

GF 13 Personal pronouns: object forms ▸ GF (pp. 138–139)

I can't do this homework. You can help **me**.
You don't know me, but I know **you**.
There's Jack. **He**'s nice. Can you see **him**?

I like **her**. Ich mag **sie**. *(Sophie, meine Lehrerin, ...)*
I like **it**. Ich mag **sie**. *(meine Schule, die Stadt, ...)*
I like **them**. Ich mag **sie**. *(meine Eltern, die Stiefel, ...)*

◂ Bei den Personalpronomen unterscheiden wir die **Subjektformen** *(I, you, he, ...)* und die **Objektformen** *(me, you, him, her, it, us, you, them)*.

! Die deutsche Objektform „sie" kann auf Englisch *her, it* oder *them* heißen.

GF 14 *some* and *any* ▸ GF (p. 139)

We've got **some** crisps and **some** cheese.
Wir haben einige Kartoffelchips und etwas Käse.

But we haven't got **any** orange juice.
Have we got **any** biscuits?
Aber wir haben keinen Orangensaft. Haben wir Kekse?

Angebot: Would you like **some** biscuits?
Bitte: Can I have **some** juice, please?

◂ *some* steht vor allem in bejahten Aussagesätzen. Es kann „einige" oder „etwas" heißen.

◂ In verneinten Aussagesätzen und in Fragen steht meist *any*.

! Wenn du mit einer Frage etwas anbietest oder um etwas bittest, verwendest du *some*.

GF 15 The simple present and the present progressive ▸ GF (p. 140)

simple present

I **help** in the kitchen **every day**.

present progressive

I'm helping in the kitchen **right now**.

Mit dem ***simple present*** (einfache Form der Gegenwart) sprichst du über das, was jemand jeden Tag tut.

Wenn du allerdings sagen möchtest, dass jemand **gerade in diesem Moment** etwas tut, musst du das ***present progressive*** (Verlaufsform der Gegenwart) verwenden.

GF 16 The present progressive ▸ GF (pp. 140–141)

a) Positive and negative statements

Sophie **is helping** in the kitchen.
Sophie hilft (gerade) in der Küche.

Das *present progressive* wird mit *am/are/is* + *-ing*-Form des Verbs gebildet: *Sophie* ***is helping***. *Emily* ***isn't helping***.

+		–	
I'm	working	I'm not	working
you're		you aren't	
he's/she's/it's		he isn't/she isn't/it isn't	
we're		we aren't	
you're		you aren't	
they're		they aren't	

b) Questions and short answers

Are you **working**, Dad? – Yes, I am. / No, I'm not.
Is Sophie's mum **making** a salad? – Yes, she is. / No, she isn't.

In Fragen sind Subjekt *(you, Sophie's mum)* und *am/are/is* vertauscht.
Die Kurzantworten sind genauso wie beim Verb *be*.

Unit 5

GF 17 The simple past ▸ GF (p. 141)

Last week Ananda **followed** Mr Green to the station.
Letzte Woche ist Ananda Mr Green zum Bahnhof gefolgt.

Mit dem *simple past* kannst du über Vergangenes berichten. Mit Zeitangaben wie *last week, yesterday, three days ago* kannst du sagen, **wann** etwas geschehen ist oder **wann** jemand etwas getan hat.

GF 18 The simple past of the verb *(to) be* ▸ GF (pp. 141–142)

Jo: The dress rehearsal **was** great.
We **were** all good.
Dan: Jack **wasn't** bad. The girls **weren't** bad.
And you **were** fantastic, Jo!
Jo: Really? **Was** I fantastic?
Dan: Well ... **no, you weren't**. Not really.

Beim *simple past* von *be* gibt es nur zwei Formen:
I, he/she/it was ***you, we, they were***

◂ Die verneinten Formen heißen ***wasn't*** und ***weren't***.

◂ Die Frage bildest du mit ***Was I ... / Were you ...?*** usw.

◂ Die Kurzantworten heißen ***Yes, I was. / No, you weren't.*** usw.

GF 19 The simple past: positive statements ▸ GF (p. 142)

a) Regular verbs

I **watched** Mr Green yesterday. Ananda **followed** him too.

Bei regelmäßigen Verben bildest du das *simple past* durch Anhängen von ***ed*** an den Infinitiv: *watch → watched, follow → followed.*

b) Irregular verbs

Lots of people went to the Spring Show.
(Infinitiv: **go**)

Wie im Deutschen gibt es auch im Englischen eine Reihe unregelmäßiger Verben, deren *simple past*-Formen du einzeln lernen musst. ▸ *Liste unregelmäßiger Verben (p. 201)*

GF 20 The simple past: negative statements ▸ GF (p. 143)

I **didn't follow** Mr Green yesterday. Ananda **didn't have** time.

Eine Aussage im *simple past* verneinst du mit ***didn't*** + **Infinitiv**.

GF 21 The simple past: questions and short answers ▸ GF (p. 143)

Did your dad **go** to the Spring Show, Jo?
– **Yes, he** did. / **No, he** didn't.

Fragen im *simple past* bildest du mit ***did***:
Did he go? (Nicht: *Did he ~~went~~?*)

Unit 6

GF 22 Extra The *going to*-future ▸ GF (p. 144)

I'**m going to find out** what Mr Green is reading.

Sophie isn't going to help Jack.

Is Ananda going to help Jack?
– Yes, she is. / No, she isn't.

Wenn du über Pläne und Absichten für die Zukunft sprechen willst, verwendest du das Futur mit ***going to***.
So wird es gebildet: ***be/am/are/is + going to*** **+ Infinitiv**
Verneinung:
I'm not/You aren't/He isn't + *going to* + Infinitiv

GF 23 Word order in subordinate clauses ▸ GF (p. 145)

I like the library **because I like books.** And I like the library **because it's quiet.**

! Anders als im Deutschen ist die Wortstellung im Nebensatz genauso wie im Hauptsatz, nämlich **Subjekt – Verb (– Objekt)**:

S	V	O		S	V	O
I	*like*	*the library*	*because*	*I*	*like*	*books*.

..., weil ich Bücher mag.

GF 24 The simple present and the present progressive in contrast ▸ GF (pp. 145–146)

Simple present:

1. Das ***simple present*** drückt aus, dass jemand etwas **wiederholt** tut:
Polly usually cleans her cage on Saturdays.
2. Das ***simple present*** wird auch verwendet, um **aufeinanderfolgende Handlungen** zu beschreiben, z.B. wenn man eine Geschichte erzählt (oft mit *First ..., then ..., after that ...*):
First Ananda follows Mr Green to the station, then she watches him. After that she calls Jack on her mobile.

Present progressive:

1. Das ***present progressive*** drückt aus, dass jemand **gerade im Moment** etwas tut:
Look, Polly is cleaning her cage now.
2. Das ***present progressive*** wird auch verwendet, um Handlungen zu beschreiben, die über einen längeren Zeitraum im Gange, also noch nicht abgeschlossen sind:
They're following and watching Mr Green.